Cambridge Preliminary English Test 2

WITH ANSWERS

Examination papers from University of Cambridge ESOL Examinations: English for Speakers of Other Languages

CAMBRIDGE
UNIVERSITY PRESS

PUBLISHED BY THE PRESS SYNDICATE OF THE UNIVERSITY OF CAMBRIDGE
The Pitt Building, Trumpington Street, Cambridge, United Kingdom

CAMBRIDGE UNIVERSITY PRESS
The Edinburgh Building, Cambridge CB2 2RU, UK
40 West 20th Street, New York NY 10011–4211, USA
477 Williamstown Road, Port Melbourne, VIC 3207, Australia
Ruiz de Alarcón 13, 28014 Madrid, Spain
Dock House, The Waterfront, Cape Town 8001, South Africa

http://www.cambridge.org

© Cambridge University Press 2003

First published 1997
New edition 2003
Reprinted 2004

Printed in the United Kingdom at the University Press, Cambridge

Typeface Helvetica 10/13. *System* QuarkXPress®   [OD&I]

A catalogue record for this book is available from the British Library

ISBN 0 521 75467 4 Student's Book with answers
ISBN 0 521 75466 6 Student's Book
ISBN 0 521 75471 2 Self-study Pack
ISBN 0 521 75468 2 Teacher's Book
ISBN 0 521 75469 0 Set of 2 Cassettes
ISBN 0 521 75470 4 Set of 2 Audio CDs

Contents

To the student   4

Test 1   6

Test 2   26

Test 3   46

Test 4   66

Test 1 Key   86

Test 2 Key   102

Test 3 Key   118

Test 4 Key   135

Sample answer sheets   152

Acknowledgements   157

Visual material for the Speaking test   *colour section I–VIII*

To the student

This book is for candidates preparing for the University of Cambridge ESOL Examinations Preliminary English Test (PET), and gives practice in all the written and oral papers. It contains four complete tests based on recent PET papers. PET tests Reading, Writing, Listening and Speaking.

PAPER 1   (1 hour and 30 minutes)

Reading
There are 35 questions in five Parts. You have to choose the right answer out of three or four options, match questions to texts or show that you think a sentence about a text is correct or incorrect.

Writing
There are three Parts: sentence transformations, a short message of 35–45 words and a letter or story of about 100 words.

PAPER 2   (about 35 minutes, including 6 minutes to transfer answers)

Listening
There are four Parts, and you will hear each of them twice. As you listen, you write your answers on the question paper. At the end, you have 6 minutes to copy your answers onto the answer sheet.

PAPER 3   (10–12 minutes for each pair of candidates)

Speaking
You take the Speaking test with another candidate. There are two examiners in the room. One examiner talks to you. This examiner sometimes asks you questions and sometimes asks you to talk to the other candidate. The other examiner listens to you. Both examiners give you marks. During the test the examiner gives you and your partner photographs and other pictures to look at and to talk about.

Preparing for PET by yourself

Reading
Have a look at some English language magazines, and read some articles about things that interest you. Look through some stories written in simplified English in your library or bookshop. Choose the ones which are interesting and just a little difficult for you, and guess the words you may not know before you look them up in your dictionary.

Writing

It can be very helpful to keep a diary in English, so that you find and learn the words that really mean something to you. You may also want to find an English-speaking penfriend or e-pal, or to exchange letters or e-mails in English with a friend who is learning with you. In those letters/e-mails you can describe something interesting you have done, what you are doing at present or talk about your plans. In that way everything you practise will be real for you and not just an exercise.

Listening

Watch any interesting English language films at your cinema, or on TV or video whenever you can. Watch or listen to any English language teaching programmes on TV or radio. (A free list of such programmes is available from the BBC, Programme Guides, Bush House, PO Box 76, London WC2B 4PH, United Kingdom.) Listen to learning materials on cassette, so that you can hear many different kinds of voices. You may also hear people speaking English in shops, restaurants or hotels, or a tourist guide telling English-speaking visitors about places of interest in your area.

Speaking

Practise talking English with a friend who is also learning, and arrange to spend time doing this regularly. Ask each other questions, tell each other what you have enjoyed doing, talk about your daily lives, your plans, your likes and dislikes – in English. It really does get easier, once you start practising!

Further information

For more information about PET or any other Cambridge ESOL examination write to:

University of Cambridge
ESOL Examinations
1 Hills Road
Cambridge
CB1 2EU
England

Telephone: +44 1223 553355
Fax: +44 1223 460278
e-mail: ESOLHelpdesk@ucles.org.uk
website: www.CambridgeESOL.org

In some areas this information can also be obtained from the British Council.

Cambridge Preliminary English Test 2
(CUP) (ISBN 0-521-75467-4)

Test 1

PAPER 1 READING AND WRITING (1 hour 30 minutes)

READING

PART 1

Questions 1–5

- Look at the text in each question.
- What does it say?
- Mark the letter next to the correct explanation – **A**, **B** or **C** – **on your answer sheet**.

Example:

0

NO BICYCLES
AGAINST GLASS
PLEASE

A Do not leave your bicycle touching the window.

B Do not ride your bicycle in this area.

C Broken glass may damage your bicycle tyres.

Example answer:

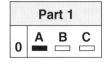

Part 1			
	A	B	C
0	■	▭	▭

1

Francesco! Problem – Maria's borrowed my history textbook and she's away. Could you lend me yours? Leave it with Ken when you see him. Thanks, Natalie

Whose textbook does Natalie want to borrow?

A Ken's

B Maria's

C Francesco's

2

THIS CAR PARK IS LOCKED AFTER BUSINESS HOURS EACH DAY

A Users must lock the car park after leaving.

B People can park here while they are at work.

C This car park is for employees only.

3

PLAYERS WANTED
for Friday's basketball match against Barton College – can YOU help the team? Come to the gym at 3 p.m. today, whatever your level.

A The basketball team only wants to see experienced players.

B There aren't enough team members available on Friday.

C The Barton College team will visit the gym later today.

4

JAZZ ON A SUMMER EVENING
NO TICKETS LEFT FOR SUNDAY'S PERFORMANCE

A All Sunday evening tickets are already sold.

B You must book tickets for Sunday in advance.

C A ticket is not necessary for Sunday evening.

5

To: Charlotte   **From:** Giacomo

What time does your flight arrive tomorrow? Can't pick you up if it's earlier than midday as I'm holding a meeting at our office – sorry.

A Giacomo will be able to see Charlotte early tomorrow morning.

B Charlotte needs to arrive in time for Giacomo's meeting tomorrow.

C Giacomo can collect Charlotte from the airport tomorrow afternoon.

PART 2

Questions 6–10

- The people below all want to go to the cinema.
- On the opposite page there are descriptions of eight films.
- Decide which film (**letters A–H**) would be the most suitable for each person or people (numbers **6–10**).
- For each of these numbers mark the correct letter **on your answer sheet**.

6 Jo is studying art at university. She usually goes to the cinema on Friday evenings. She enjoys films that are based on real life and from which she can learn something.

7  Sheila has decided to take her mother to the cinema for her birthday. They both like love stories that have happy endings.

8 Brian is a hard-working medical student. He doesn't have very much free time, but he likes going to the cinema to relax, and enjoys a good laugh.

9  Adam wants to take his 8-year-old son Mark to the cinema at the weekend. They want to see a film with plenty of excitement.

10  Harry and Joyce go to the cinema about twice a month. They particularly like detective stories and do not pay much attention to which actors are in the film.

A *The Delivery*

Jim Treace stars in this well-known comedy about two workmen who have to deliver a long piece of wood to a house. But unfortunately the performances are poor, and the film is too long for such a simple joke.

B *And Tomorrow We Find You*

A fast-moving adult story about a San Francisco policeman in danger. Based on a real-life happening, it keeps you guessing right until the last minute. Although there are no big stars, there are some fine performances.

C *The Ends of the Earth*

A story based on a real-life journey to the South Pole. This film contains some quite wonderful wildlife photography – make sure you see it while you have the chance, or you'll be sorry.

D *Island of Fire*

You get spectacular scenery and lots of thrills in this action-packed story, in which a young sea-captain rescues terrified villagers from a volcanic island in the South Seas.

E *Out of School*

Here we live through a day in the life of an American teenager who has problems not only with his parents and their boring friends but also with his first girlfriend who just doesn't seem to understand him.

F *A Time of Silence*

Don't forget your handkerchief for this story of a young college boy and girl who manage to survive all the pressures of modern life. And what an unforgettable wedding scene!

G *A Private Party*

A wonderfully funny comedy, which takes place in the 1940s. A reporter and his very worried wife try to save a sheep from the local butcher. The actors really make the most of this clever script.

H Who Shot Malone?

It's a surprise to see so many famous names wasting their time in this dull detective story. In the end you find yourself asking, 'Who cares?'

PART 3

Questions 11–20

- Look at the sentences below about a tour of Australia.
- Read the text on the opposite page to decide if each sentence is correct or incorrect.
- If it is correct, mark **A on your answer sheet**.
- If it is not correct, mark **B on your answer sheet**.

11   If you start your holiday on April 1st, you will return on April 19th.

12   Return flights are from Melbourne.

13   All travel between cities in Australia is by plane.

14   The cost covers accommodation and some meals.

15   You can make a reservation now for one of next year's tours.

16   You have to pay the full price on the day you book.

17   You can only take this holiday in the spring or autumn.

18   If you want to go on a city sightseeing tour, you will have to pay extra.

19   The trip to Ayers Rock ends with a flight.

20   Booking is possible seven days a week.

GLOBEWISE
WE'll SHOW YOU THE VERY BEST OF
AUSTRALIA
ON A FULLY GUIDED 22-DAY TOUR

BOOK NOW

for only
£1985

OUR PRICE INCLUDES

- *Scheduled flights by Australia's national airline, Quantas, from London or Manchester to Perth, returning from Melbourne.*
- *After arriving in Perth, Air Australia flights between Perth/Alice Springs/Cairns/ Sydney.*
- *Coach from Sydney to Melbourne via Canberra and Albury.*
- *All airport transfers in Australia.*
- *Nineteen nights' accommodation in good grade hotels with full continental breakfast.*
- *Day trip to Ayers Rock, with a full day Barrier Reef boat trip, a visit to an Australian sheep station and city sightseeing tours in Perth, Alice Springs, Sydney, Canberra and Melbourne.*
- *All state and local taxes.*
- *Hotel baggage handling.*
- *Experienced Globewise Tour Manager at all stages of the trip.*

SOLD OUT FOR THIS YEAR BOOKING NOW FOR NEXT YEAR

You can pay just £90 now to be sure of your place on this successful and popular touring holiday next year.
There are departures right through the year. We make sure you see the very best of everything which Australia has to offer.

PERTH
Wonderful long, golden beaches, superb restaurants serving fabulous food in delightful surroundings, lush green parks and the beautiful Swan River. City sightseeing tour included.

ALICE SPRINGS
Fly over the outback to famous Alice Springs in the heart of Aboriginal country. Full sightseeing tour. See Flying Doctor base and 'School of the Air'.

AYERS ROCK
Drive to Yulara National Park. Visit the mysterious Olgas and Ayers Rock with its caves and Aboriginal rock paintings. Fly on to the lively seaside town of Cairns and relax in the sun.

GREAT BARRIER REEF
We've included a full day's boat trip on the famous reef with the chance to see amazing, brightly coloured fish and other sea creatures.

SYDNEY
You'll love the excitement and beauty of Australia's biggest city – we've included a sightseeing tour and a visit to the famous Opera House. You can also book a day trip to the Blue Mountains.

MELBOURNE
We've included a city sightseeing tour – or you can visit the Penguin Parade.
We promise that by the end of the trip you'll be wanting to return!

PHONE US ON 01303 692154

QUOTING REFERENCE **GW/398** FOR OUR NEW FULL COLOUR BROCHURE

OUR OFFICES ARE OPEN:
Monday to Friday
9 a.m. – 8 p.m.
Saturday
9 a.m. – 4 p.m.

BROCHURE REQUESTS ONLY:
Sunday
10 a.m. – 2 p.m.

PART 4

Questions 21–25

- Read the text and questions below.
- For each question, mark the letter next to the correct answer – **A**, **B**, **C** or **D** –
  on your answer sheet.

A month ago I had no idea that on a Saturday afternoon in November I'd be hanging 30 metres above the ground and enjoying it. Now I looked down at the river far below me, and realised why people love rock-climbing.

My friend Matt and I had arrived at the Activity Centre on Friday evening. The accommodation wasn't wonderful, but we had everything we needed (beds, blankets, food), and we were pleased to be out of the city and in the fresh air.

On Saturday morning we met the other ten members of our group. Cameron had come along with two friends, Kevin and Simon, while sisters Carole and Lynn had come with Amanda. We had come from various places and none of us knew the area.

We knew we were going to spend the weekend outdoors, but none of us was sure exactly how. Half of us spent the morning caving while the others went rock-climbing and then we changed at lunchtime. Matt and I went to the caves first. Climbing out was harder than going in, but after a good deal of pushing, we were out at last – covered in mud but pleased and excited by what we'd done.

---

21 What is the writer trying to do in the text?

    A   advertise the Activity Centre

    B   describe some people she met

    C   explain how to do certain outdoor sports

    D   say how she spent some free time

22 What can the reader learn from the text?

    A   when to depend on other people at the Centre

    B   how to apply for a place at the Centre

    C   what sort of activities you can experience at the Centre

    D   which time of year is best to attend the Centre

23 How do you think the writer might describe her weekend?

A interesting
B relaxing
C frightening
D unpleasant

24 What do we learn about the group?

A Some of them had been there before.
B They had already chosen their preferred activities.
C Some of them already knew each other.
D They came from the same city.

25 Which of the following advertisements describes the Activity Centre?

A

> ACTIVITY CENTRE
> Set in beautiful countryside.
> Accommodation and meals provided.
> Make up your own timetable – choose
> from a variety of activities (horse-
> riding, fishing, hill-walking, sailing,
> mountain-biking).

B

> ACTIVITY CENTRE
> Set in beautiful countryside.
> Accommodation provided. Work with
> a group – we show you a range of
> outdoor activities that you didn't
> realise you could do!

C

> ACTIVITY CENTRE
> Set in beautiful countryside. Enjoy the
> luxury of our accommodation – each
> room has its own bathroom. Work
> with a group, or have individual
> teaching.

D

> ACTIVITY CENTRE
> Set in beautiful countryside. You can
> spend the day doing outdoor activities
> and we will find your accommodation
> with a local family.

PART 5

Questions 26–35

- Read the text below and choose the correct word for each space.
- For each question, mark the letter next to the correct word – **A**, **B**, **C** or **D** – on **your answer sheet**.

Example answer:

	Part 5
0	A ▬ B ☐ C ☐ D ☐

THE FIRST WOMAN SCIENTIST

Hypatia was **(0)** .... in Alexandria, in Egypt, in 370 A.D. For many centuries she was **(26)** .... only woman scientist to have a place in the history books.

Hypatia's father was director of Alexandria University, and he **(27)** .... sure his daughter had the best education available. This was unusual, as most women then had few **(28)** .... to study.

After studying in Athens and Rome, Hypatia returned to Alexandria **(29)** .... she began teaching mathematics. She soon became famous **(30)** .... her knowledge of new ideas.

We have no copies of her books, **(31)** .... we know that she wrote several important mathematical works. Hypatia was also interested in technology and **(32)** .... several scientific tools to help with her work.

At the **(33)** .... many rulers were afraid of science, and **(34)** .... connected with it was in danger. One day in March 415, Hypatia **(35)** .... attacked in the street and killed.

0	**A** born	**B** begun	**C** developed	**D** grown
26	**A** one	**B** the	**C** a	**D** an
27	**A** could	**B** made	**C** said	**D** put
28	**A** classes	**B** customs	**C** opportunities	**D** teachers
29	**A** where	**B** how	**C** there	**D** which
30	**A** from	**B** by	**C** for	**D** in
31	**A** because	**B** but	**C** or	**D** as
32	**A** did	**B** experimented	**C** invented	**D** learnt
33	**A** day	**B** period	**C** year	**D** time
34	**A** anyone	**B** nobody	**C** all	**D** something
35	**A** was	**B** had	**C** has	**D** is

WRITING

PART 1

Questions 1–5

- Here are some questions about a family.
- For each question complete the second sentence so that it means the same as the first, **using no more than three words**.
- **Write only the missing words on your answer sheet.**

      Example: My brother is older than me.

                I am .*younger than*. **my brother.**

1   My parents prefer jazz to classical music.

     My parents think jazz .... **than classical music.**

2   My parents can only go swimming at the weekend.

     On weekdays, my parents aren't .... **go swimming.**

3   If I finish my homework, I can go out at the weekend.

     I can't go out at the weekend .... **finish my homework.**

4   My sister watches more TV than me.

     I don't watch TV .... **my sister does.**

5   My parents suggested going out for a meal.

     My parents said, 'Why .... **we go out for a meal?'**

PART 2

Question 6

You have invited your English friend Jo to stay with you next month, but you now need to delay this visit.

Write a card to send to Jo. In your card, you should

- apologise to Jo
- explain why the visit has to be delayed
- suggest when it would be convenient for Jo to come.

Write 35–45 words on your answer sheet.

PART 3

Answer **one** of the following questions (**7** or **8**).

Question 7

- Your English teacher has asked you to write a story.
- Your story must begin with this sentence:

Carla looked at the car in surprise.

- Write your **story** in about 100 words **on your answer sheet**.

Question 8

- This is part of a letter you receive from an English friend.

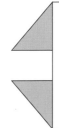

> I know you often go to the cinema. Tell me about the last film you saw and whether you enjoyed it.

- Now write a letter to your friend.
- Write your **letter** in about 100 words **on your answer sheet**.

Cambridge Preliminary English Test 2
(CUP) (ISBND-521-75467-4)

PAPER 2   LISTENING about 35 minutes
(including 6 minutes transfer time)

PART 1

Questions 1–7

- There are seven questions in this part.
- For each question there are three pictures and a short recording.
- Choose the correct picture and put a tick (✓) in the box below it.

Example: What's the time?

A ✓   B ☐   C ☐

1   Where will the girls meet?

A ☐   B ☐   C ☐

2   Which chair does the man want?

A ☐   B ☐   C ☐

3   Which picture shows what the girls need?

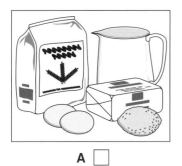   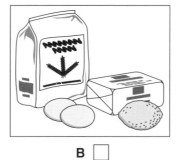   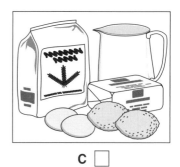

A ☐   B ☐   C ☐

4   Which picture shows what happened?

A ☐   B ☐   C ☐

5   What is Sarah's mother doing?

A ☐   B ☐   C ☐

6 What luggage is the man taking on holiday?

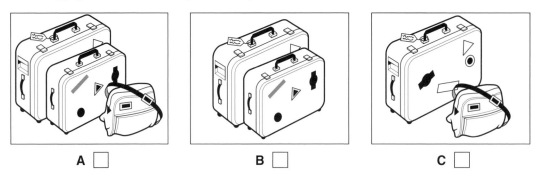

A ☐   B ☐   C ☐

7 Which photograph does the man like?

A ☐   B ☐   C ☐

PART 2

Questions 8–13

- You will hear part of a radio programme about classical music.
- For each question, put a tick (✓) in the correct box.

8 This week's prize is

A ☐ a music cassette.

B ☐ two concert tickets.

C ☐ a classical CD.

9 The person who wrote the music lived in

A ☐ Italy.

B ☐ Spain.

C ☐ France.

10 What else shares the title of this music?

A ☐ a garden

B ☐ a play

C ☐ a park

11 What did people do when they first heard the music?

A ☐ Some left before the end.

B ☐ Only a few clapped.

C ☐ Some asked for their money back.

12 This piece of music has been

A ☐ played in the cinema.

B ☐ used in advertising.

C ☐ used for a TV play.

13 If you know the competition answer you should ring

A ☐ 0108 937 224.

B ☐ 0018 739 242.

C ☐ 0018 937 224.

PART 3

Questions 14–19

- You will hear a radio programme in which young people from different parts of the country are interviewed.
- For each question, fill in the missing information in the numbered space.

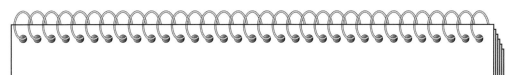

Information sheet

Name: *Mike Davis*

Age: *13 years*

Favourite subject: **(14)** ....

Favourite sport: **(15)** ....

Usual transport: **(16)** ....

On Saturday: **(17)** ....

On **(18)** .... : *Young Farmers' Group*

Future job: **(19)** ....

PART 4

Questions 20–25

- Look at the six sentences for this part.
- You will hear a conversation between a boy, Jim, and his mother.
- Decide if each sentence is correct or incorrect.
- If it is correct, put a tick (✓) in the box under **A** for **YES**. If it is not correct, put a tick (✓) in the box under **B** for **NO**.

		A YES	B NO
20	Jim's bicycle needs to be mended.	☐	☐
21	He's keen to start saving money.	☐	☐
22	His mother thinks a mountain bike is suitable for their area.	☐	☐
23	She encourages Jim to manage his money better.	☐	☐
24	His mother offers to lend him some money.	☐	☐
25	Jim is disappointed by his mother's suggestion.	☐	☐

About the Speaking test

The Speaking test lasts about 10 to 12 minutes. You take the test with another candidate. There are two examiners in the room. One examiner talks to you and the other examiner listens to you. Both the examiners give you marks.

Part 1

The examiners introduce themselves and then one examiner asks you and your partner to say your names and spell them. This examiner then asks you questions about yourself, your daily life, interests, etc.

Part 2

The examiner asks you to talk about something together and gives you a drawing to help you.

Part 3

You each have a chance to talk by yourselves. The examiner gives you a colour photograph to look at and asks you to talk about it. When you have finished talking, the examiner gives your partner a different photograph to look at and to talk about.

Part 4

The examiner asks you and your partner to say more about the subject of the photographs in Part 3. You may be asked to give your opinion or to talk about something that has happened to you.

Test 2

PAPER 1   READING AND WRITING   (1 hour 30 minutes)

READING

PART 1

Questions 1–5

- Look at the text in each question.
- What does it say?
- Mark the letter next to the correct explanation – **A**, **B** or **C** – **on your answer sheet**.

Example:

0

> **NO BICYCLES**
> **AGAINST GLASS**
> **PLEASE**

A Do not leave your bike touching the window.

B Do not ride your bicycle in this area.

C Broken glass may damage your bicycle tyres.

Example answer:

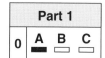

	Part 1		
0	A	B	C

1

> LUGGAGE CANNOT
> BE REMOVED
> WITHOUT A RECEIPT

A You must show a receipt if you want to remove luggage.

B When you remove your luggage you are given a receipt.

C You can leave your luggage here without change.

2

☎ **Message**

Anna,
Jeff rang: suggests taking a blanket
(cold there!) No need to bring
programme now. He'll meet you at the
festival entrance with your ticket.

For the festival, Anna should bring

A her ticket.

B a blanket.

C the programme.

3

**Will the last person
to leave please
switch off the lights**

A Don't turn the lights on until it's necessary.

B Switch the lights on when you're in the room.

C Don't leave the lights on if the room is empty.

4

Has anyone seen my gold chain?
I took it off before athletics. It's a
present from my boyfriend – he
mustn't find out it's lost!

Sally

A Sally has given a chain to someone as a present.

B Sally's boyfriend knows about the missing chain.

C Sally lost her chain when she got changed for sport.

5

*Assistants needed
because of new
opening hours –
apply inside*

This shop

A has just opened and jobs are available.

B is opening for longer and needs extra staff.

C will open late because of job interviews.

PART 2

Questions 6–10

- The people below all want to buy a book on travel.
- On the opposite page there are descriptions of eight books.
- Decide which book (**letters A–H**) would be the most suitable for each person or people (**numbers 6–10**).
- For each of these numbers mark the correct letter **on your answer sheet**.

6  Robert is planning to travel round the world by train. He would like a book with pictures and maps to take with him on his long journeys.

7  Mrs Jones used to love visiting France, but now she is too old to travel. She wants a book with lots of photographs which will help her to remember everything she enjoyed.

8  The Harpers are planning to go on holiday round Europe. They intend to drive their car and go for walks, so they need a book with maps and pictures to guide them on their way.

9  Clive wants to buy a book as a present for his friend Tom. Tom enjoys fishing and driving round England.

10  Peter has to write something for his history teacher about world explorers. He wants to know about explorers from the past and their travels to different parts of the world.

A Allan Jowett

Jowett's Railway Centres: Volume 1

Packed with information about 20 British railway centres, this wonderful book is handwritten and illustrated throughout with clear hand-drawn maps – a true collector's piece for those who are interested in railways.

B Alan Titchmarsh

The English River

Alan Titchmarsh explores 18 rivers, telling their interesting stories with his appreciation of them. A saying from a past age introduces each chapter as his exploration moves across the English countryside.

C Robin Hanbury-Tenison

The Oxford Book of Exploration

This is a collection of the writing of explorers through the centuries. It describes the feelings and experiences of these brave adventurers who changed the world through their search for new lands.

D The Travel Club

Train Journeys of the World

First-hand accounts of 30 of the world's most beautiful and dramatic railway journeys are found together with specially drawn maps and wonderful photographs that show the people and places on the route.

E Bruce Chatwin

Photographs and Notebooks

On all his travels, Bruce Chatwin took thousands of photographs and kept daily notebooks. Published here for the first time, the photographs are excellent, the notebooks both scholarly and funny. Will give great pleasure.

F Automobile Association

Walks and Tours in France

Explore spectacular and pretty France with 61 expertly researched motor tours and 114 walks, complete with route directions, super mapping, and descriptions and pictures of places of interest for the traveller.

G Shirley Pike

The Book of French Life

This beautiful volume contains forty wonderful photographs that show the very nature of French life – the perfect gift for anyone who finds this country as wonderful as Shirley Pike does.

H Ranulph Fiennes
Mind over Matter

The epic crossing of the Antarctic continent

The amazing story of his recent crossing of the Antarctic continent with another explorer, in which both showed great strength and courage.

PART 3

Questions 11–20

- Look at the sentences below about a river journey.
- Read the text on the opposite page to decide if each sentence is correct or incorrect.
- If it is correct, mark **A on your answer sheet**.
- If it is not correct, mark **B on your answer sheet**.

11 Each cabin on the *Lady Ivy May* is for two people.

12 You can borrow books on board the ship.

13 On arrival at Oporto, guests find their own way to the ship.

14 You spend a day looking round Oporto.

15 It takes a day to travel from Oporto to Entre-os-Rios.

16 The museum at Lamego used to be a palace.

17 It is sometimes possible for the *Lady Ivy May* to sail to the Spanish border.

18 The trip includes some travel by train.

19 You arrive back in Oporto on the day before your return flight.

20 *Voyages Jules Verne* arrange your travel insurance.

A JOURNEY ALONG THE BEAUTIFUL DOURO RIVER

7 nights from £1050

VOYAGES JULES VERNE operate a 'hotel ship' along the Douro river in Portugal. The MV *Lady Ivy May* can take 160 guests in double cabins, all of which face outside and have a private shower and WC. On board the ship, which has air-conditioning, you will find a sun-deck, lounge, bar, dining room, shop and library facilities.

Itinerary

Day 1 Depart in the early evening from London Heathrow to Oporto. Your guide will meet you on arrival and take you to the *Lady Ivy May*, where you will spend the night.

Day 2 After a morning's sightseeing in Oporto, you will return to the ship and depart for Entre-os-Rios. This part of the journey up the river takes four hours.

Day 3 You will continue travelling up the river. In the early evening, the ship stops at Pêso da Régua, where port wine is produced. At dinner you will be able to try the delicious food and drink from this area.

Day 4 After breakfast you will travel south by bus to the ancient town of Lamego and visit the cathedral, several churches and a museum. The museum was formerly a palace and now has an excellent collection of paintings, tapestries and sculptures. You will then return to the ship and sail on to Tua.

Day 5 At this point the Douro becomes very narrow. Depending on the depth of the river at the time, you may be able to continue by a smaller boat to the Spanish frontier at Barca d'Alva. The return journey to Tua is by coach and there is much to see along the way.

Day 6 In the morning you will drive to São João da Pesqueira for one of the most wonderful views in the whole of the Douro valley. You will return to the ship for lunch and then join the Douro river valley railway for a beautiful ride through the countryside to Régua, where the *Lady Ivy May* will be waiting for you.

Day 7 There will be a trip to Vila Real before returning to the ship for lunch and then setting off down the river to Oporto. You will sleep on board the *Lady Ivy May*.

Day 8 You will arrive in Oporto in plenty of time for independent sightseeing and last-minute shopping, before you catch the flight home to London Heathrow.

Departure dates and prices

(all prices are per person)

June 5, 12, 19, 26	**£1100**
July 3, 10, 17, 24, 31	**£1050**
August 7, 14, 21, 28	**£1050**
September 4, 11, 18, 25	**£1100**

Prices include:

return flights, 7 nights' accommodation on board the *Lady Ivy May* with all meals, excursions and guides.

Not included:

travel insurance, tips.

Voyages Jules Verne

PART 4

Questions 21–25

- Read the text and questions below.
- For each question, mark the letter next to the correct answer – **A**, **B**, **C** or **D** – **on your answer sheet**.

Winter Driving

Winter is dangerous because it's so difficult to know what is going to happen and accidents take place so easily. Fog can be waiting to meet you over the top of a hill. Ice might be hiding beneath the melting snow, waiting to send you off the road. The car coming towards you may suddenly slide across the road.

Rule Number One for driving on icy roads is to drive smoothly. Uneven movements can make a car suddenly very difficult to control. So every time you either turn the wheel, touch the brakes or increase your speed, you must be as gentle and slow as possible. Imagine you are driving with a full cup of hot coffee on the seat next to you. Drive so that you wouldn't spill it.

Rule Number Two is to pay attention to what might happen. The more ice there is, the further down the road you have to look. Test how long it takes to stop by gently braking. Remember that you may be driving more quickly than you think. In general, allow double your normal stopping distance when the road is wet, three times this distance on snow, and even more on ice. Try to stay in control of your car at all times and you will avoid trouble.

21 What is the writer trying to do in the text?

    A   complain about bad winter driving
    B   give information about winter weather
    C   warn people against driving in winter
    D   advise people about safe driving in winter

22 Why would somebody read this text?

    A   to find out about the weather
    B   for information on driving lessons
    C   to learn about better driving
    D   to decide when to travel

23 What does the writer think?

    A   People should avoid driving in the snow.
    B   Drivers should expect problems in winter.
    C   People drive too fast in winter.
    D   Winter drivers should use their brakes less.

24 Why does the writer talk about a cup of coffee?

    A   to explain the importance of smooth movements
    B   because he thinks refreshments are important for drivers
    C   because he wants drivers to be more relaxed
    D   to show how it can be spilled

25 Which traffic sign shows the main idea of the text?

A
DRIVE CAREFULLY

ICE ON ROAD
AHEAD

B
**REDUCE SPEED
NOW**

FOG AHEAD

C
DRIVE CAREFULLY

ROAD REPAIRS
AHEAD

D
SLOW DOWN

ACCIDENT
AHEAD

PART 5

Questions 26–35

- Read the text below and choose the correct word for each space.
- For each question, mark the letter next to the correct word – **A**, **B**, **C** or **D** – **on your answer sheet**.

Example answer:

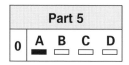

SAMUEL PEPYS

The most famous diary **(0)** .... English was written by Samuel Pepys. It gives a detailed and interesting **(26)** .... of everyday life in England **(27)** .... 1660 and 1669. Pepys writes about important news stories of the time, like disease, an enemy navy **(28)** .... up the River Thames and the Great Fire of London.

   He also writes about himself, even about his **(29)** .... – he often slept during church or **(30)** .... at the pretty girls. He describes his home life – a **(31)** .... with his wife and how they became friends again, his worry about her illness. As well as books, he liked music, the theatre, card **(32)** .... , and parties with good food and **(33)** .... of fun. Pepys was a busy man who had many important **(34)** .... – he was a Member of Parliament and President of the Royal Society. He is also **(35)** .... for his work for the British Navy.

0	A in	B about	C from	D of
26	A description	B letter	C notice	D story
27	A between	B from	C through	D to
28	A driving	B flying	C running	D sailing
29	A accidents	B plans	C dreams	D faults
30	A looked	B prayed	C talked	D thought
31	A conversation	B discussion	C quarrel	D talk
32	A battles	B games	C matches	D plays
33	A amount	B plenty	C much	D some
34	A acts	B hobbies	C jobs	D studies
35	A reviewed	B remembered	C reminded	D reported

WRITING

PART 1

Questions 1–5

- Here are some sentences about going to the supermarket.
- For each question, complete the second sentence so that it means the same as the first, **using no more than three words**.
- **Write only the missing words on your answer sheet.**

Example: My mother lives a long way from the supermarket.

There isn't *a supermarket near* **my mother's house.**

1   When she has to walk to the supermarket she finds it tiring.

She gets .... **when she has to walk to the supermarket.**

2   She is often driven to the supermarket by her neighbour.

Her neighbour often .... **a lift to the supermarket.**

3   There are many types of coffee there.

You can buy a .... **types of coffee there.**

4   She asked an assistant how much the Colombian coffee cost.

She asked: 'How .... **the Colombian coffee cost?'**

5   The Colombian coffee cost less than the Kenyan coffee.

The Colombian coffee wasn't .... **as the Kenyan coffee.**

PART 2

Question 6

You have just had a wonderful holiday staying with some English-speaking friends in the countryside.

Write an e-mail to your friends. In your e-mail, you should

- thank them for your stay
- say what you most enjoyed about the countryside
- suggest where you could meet each other next time.

Write 35–45 words on your answer sheet.

PART 3

Answer **one** of the following questions (**7** or **8**).

Question 7

- This is part of a letter you receive from your penfriend.

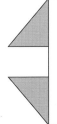 In your next letter, could you give me some advice? Tell me how you keep fit and healthy!

- Now write a letter to your penfriend.
- Write your **letter** in about 100 words **on your answer sheet**.

Question 8

- You have to write a story for your English homework.
- Your story must have this title:

An exciting adventure

- Write your **story** in about 100 words **on your answer sheet**.

PAPER 2   LISTENING   about 35 minutes
(including 6 minutes transfer time)

PART 1

Questions 1–7

- There are seven questions in this part.
- For each question there are three pictures and a short recording.
- Choose the correct picture and put a tick (✓) in the box below it.

Example: What's the time?

A ✓   B ☐   C ☐

1   When and where are they meeting?

A ☐   B ☐   C ☐

2   What will Chris get for his birthday?

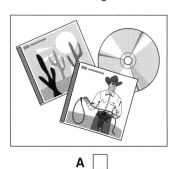      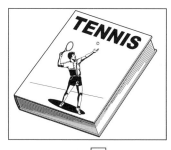

A ☐   B ☐   C ☐

3 What does Mr Jones look like?

A ☐   B ☐   C ☐

4 Where is he going to plant the tree?

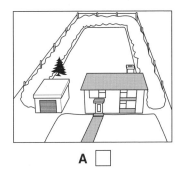 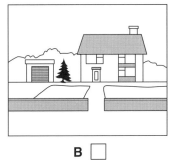 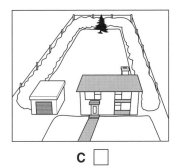

A ☐   B ☐   C ☐

5 What is the man going to buy?

 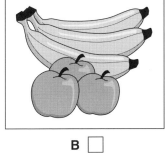 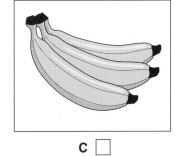

A ☐   B ☐   C ☐

6 Which is Gary's room?

A ☐   B ☐   C ☐

7 Which is the best vehicle for the man?

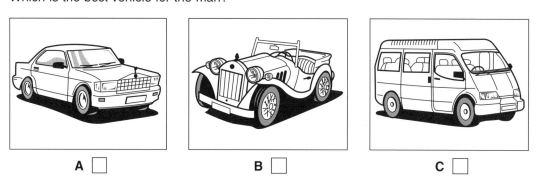

A ☐   B ☐   C ☐

PART 2

Questions 8–13

- You will hear a recorded message about an arts festival.
- For each question, put a tick (✓) in the correct box.

8   The festival takes place from

    A ☐ 12 to 18 May.

    B ☐ 12 to 20 May.

    C ☐ 12 to 28 May.

9   What is on at the Theatre Royal on 19 May?

    A ☐ jazz

    B ☐ opera

    C ☐ classical music

10   During lunchtime jazz concerts at the Corn Exchange they sell

    A ☐ soft drinks and sandwiches.

    B ☐ wine and sandwiches.

    C ☐ soft drinks and light meals.

11   What is on at the cathedral?

    A ☐ music

    B ☐ poetry

    C ☐ films

12 What does the festival programme offer at Ickworth?

    A ☐ a walk and a book reading

    B ☐ a concert and a meal

    C ☐ a walk and a concert

13 You can't use a credit card if you book

    A ☐ by post.

    B ☐ by fax.

    C ☐ by telephone.

PART 3

Questions 14–19

- You will hear someone talking on the radio about a Language Study Fair.
- For each question, fill in the missing information in the numbered space.

The Language Study Fair

Dates: 17th to 19th (**14**) ....

Place: National Education Centre

Fair includes: ● stands with textbooks

                        ● (**15**) .... by educational speakers

                        ● exhibition of furniture

                        ● demonstrations of latest (**16**) ....

Opening hours: 9.30 a.m.–5.00 p.m. Thursday and Friday

                        9.30 a.m.–4.00 p.m (**17**) ....

Tickets: £5

                        or £3 for (**18**) ....

Tickets can be booked by ringing the hotline on (19) ....

PART 4

Questions 20–25

- Look at the six sentences for this part.
- You will hear a conversation between a girl, Kate, and a boy, George.
- Decide if each sentence is correct or incorrect.
- If it is correct, put a tick (✓) in the box under **A** for **YES**. If it is not correct, put a tick (✓) in the box under **B** for **NO**.

		A YES	B NO
20	Kate has stopped taking her medicine.	☐	☐
21	George thinks Kate should stay away from class.	☐	☐
22	Kate had an accident on her bike last week.	☐	☐
23	George thinks Mr Gray is a lazy lecturer.	☐	☐
24	Kate will miss three lectures.	☐	☐
25	Kate wants to stay at home at the weekend.	☐	☐

About the Speaking test

The Speaking test lasts about 10 to 12 minutes. You take the test with another candidate. There are two examiners in the room. One examiner talks to you and the other examiner listens to you. Both the examiners give you marks.

Part 1

The examiners introduce themselves and then one examiner asks you and your partner to say your names and spell them. This examiner then asks you questions about yourself, your daily life, interests, etc.

Part 2

The examiner asks you to talk about something together and gives you a drawing to help you.

Part 3

You each have a chance to talk by yourselves. The examiner gives you a colour photograph to look at and asks you to talk about it. When you have finished talking, the examiner gives your partner a different photograph to look at and to talk about.

Part 4

The examiner asks you and your partner to say more about the subject of the photographs in Part 3. You may be asked to give your opinion or to talk about something that has happened to you.

Test 3

PAPER 1   READING AND WRITING   (1 hour 30 minutes)

READING

PART 1

Questions 1–5

- Look at the text in each question.
- What does it say?
- Mark the letter next to the correct explanation – **A**, **B** or **C** – **on your answer sheet**.

Example:

0

NO BICYCLES AGAINST GLASS PLEASE

A   Do not leave your bicycle touching the window.

B   Do not ride your bicycle in this area.

C   Broken glass may damage your bicycle tyres.

Example answer:

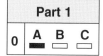

1

To: All students
From: College Secretary

Monday 6 May
Can I remind you that all essays are due this Friday. No late work will be accepted unless accompanied by a doctor's letter.

A   The college secretary will post students their essays on Friday.

B   Students may hand in their essays after Friday if they can prove illness.

C   Unless your essay is due by Friday, you do not need to reply.

2

A Take the tablets regularly until the bottle is empty.

B Take one tablet every day until they are finished.

C Take three tablets after meals until you feel better.

3

Kim suggests

A meeting at the football match.

B going to Ben's house later.

C playing on his brother's computer.

4

FREE SOFA!
(Owner moving back to New Zealand)

Must have transport – collect from John any evening this week. Phone 452611 to arrange a suitable time.

A John can deliver the sofa if the time is convenient.

B Anyone wanting this sofa must pick it up this week.

C Call John with advice on how he can transport his sofa.

5

The hire charge covers all the costs

A including fuel and insurance.

B except insurance.

C apart from fuel.

PART 2

Questions 6–10

- The people below all want to come to Britain to study English.
- On the opposite page there are descriptions of eight colleges.
- Decide which college (**letters A–H**) would be the most suitable for each person (**numbers 6–10**).
- For each of these numbers mark the correct letter **on your answer sheet**.

6  Marta wants a course in Business Studies and English, starting in September. She would prefer to be in a city, but wants a college which will organise visits, so she can see something of Britain.

7 Jean wants to attend classes for a few hours a week in July, so that he has plenty of free time to visit the countryside. He wants to stay in a city, with a family.

8  Laura is looking for a full-time beginners' course and can come to Britain at any time. She is keen on sport and wants to stay with a family.

9 Marek likes big cities. He hopes to find work during the day, so he is looking for an evening class. He wants to live in a flat or house.

10 Birgit is going to spend August in Britain. She knows some English already and wants a full-time course. She wants to meet people through the college and live with a family.

A Lowton College

Situated in a pleasant area of the city close to the river. Convenient for North Wales and the English Lake District.

- Courses in English run all year.
- Part-time courses available in the evenings/days.
- We will arrange accommodation with an English family.

B Bristow College

The college is in the centre of Bristow.

- ◆ Full-time courses at all levels, beginners to advanced, from September to June.
- ◆ Visits arranged to places of interest.
- ◆ Excellent range of sports offered.
- ◆ Students arrange their own accommodation in flats and houses.

C Shepton College

Shepton College is in the centre of London close to underground and buses.

- ☆ Classes are offered all through the year.
- ☆ Daytime English courses up to ten hours per week. Evening classes of four hours per week.
- ☆ Extra classes offered in English for Business.
- ☆ Students arrange their own accommodation in flats and houses.

D Frampton College

Situated in West London close to bus and underground.

- ✿ *Courses run from September to July (daytime only).*
- ✿ *Special courses available, e.g. English for Business.*
- ✿ *Summer school in July and August.*
- ✿ *Accommodation arranged in student hostels.*

E Daunston College

Daunston is a small town in the Midlands near pleasant countryside.

- ■ Part-time and full-time classes available from September to June.
- ■ Full-time summer school in August.
- ■ Complete beginners part-time only.
- ■ Trips and other social events arranged regularly.
- ■ Accommodation in the college or with families.

F Exford College

Exford is beside the sea and surrounded by beautiful countryside.

- ➤ Courses at all levels, September to June (full-time).
- ➤ Summer schools (mornings only) during August.
- ➤ Full social programme including sports and hobby clubs provided by the college.
- ➤ Students live in college rooms or with families.

G *Chesford College*

Situated in the centre of Chesford, a quiet market town.

- ◇ English courses offered from September to June, daytime and evenings.
- ◇ Trips organised to Cambridge, Oxford and London.
- ◇ Accommodation is with local families.

H Howe College

The college is in the city centre, but near the North Yorkshire countryside and the sea.

- Classes run from September to June.
- Part-time and full-time courses from beginners to advanced (daytime only).
- Full-time courses in English with Business Studies.
- Trips arranged to places of interest.
- Help given in finding a flat or room in the area.

PART 3

Questions 11–20

- Look at the sentences below about an English city.
- Read the text on the opposite page to decide if each sentence is correct or incorrect.
- If it is correct, mark **A on your answer sheet**.
- If it is not correct, mark **B on your answer sheet**.

11 The River Wensum flows through East Anglia.

12 People have lived by the River Wensum for at least 2000 years.

13 In the 11th century, Norwich was a small village.

14 Norwich has been a city since its first cathedral was built.

15 Norwich has always been one of the smallest English cities.

16 There are more than 50 churches in Norwich.

17 The number of students in Norwich is increasing.

18 The Norwich City football team is called 'The Canaries' because of the colours the players wear.

19 'The Castle Mall' took more than two years to build.

20 Norwich people still like using the old market as well as shopping in 'The Castle Mall'.

Norwich

Norwich, the capital of the part of Britain known as East Anglia, has existed as a place to live for more than two thousand years. It began as a small village beside the River Wensum. At the time of the Norman invasion in 1066 it had grown to become one of the largest towns in England.

With two cathedrals and a mosque, Norwich has long been a popular centre for various religions. The first cathedral was built in 1095 and has recently celebrated its 900th anniversary, while Norwich itself had a year of celebration in 1994 to mark the 800th anniversary of the city receiving a Royal Charter. This allowed it to be called a city and to govern itself independently.

Today, in comparison with places like London or Manchester, Norwich is quite small, with a population of around 150,000, but in the 16th century Norwich was the second city of England. It continued to grow for the next 300 years and got richer and richer, becoming famous for having as many churches as there are weeks in the year and as many pubs as there are days in the year.

Nowadays, there are far fewer churches and pubs, but in 1964 the University of East Anglia was built in Norwich. With its fast-growing student population and its success as a modern commercial centre (Norwich is the biggest centre for insurance services outside London), the city now has a wide choice of entertainment: theatres, cinemas, nightclubs, busy cafés, excellent restaurants, and a number of arts and leisure centres. There is also a football team, whose colours are green and yellow. The team is known as 'The Canaries', though nobody can be sure why.

Now the city's attractions include another important development, a modern shopping centre called 'The Castle Mall'. The people of Norwich lived with a very large hole in the middle of their city for over two years, as builders dug up the main car park. Lorries moved nearly a million tons of earth so that the roof of the Mall could become a city centre park, with attractive water pools and hundreds of trees. But the local people are really pleased that the old open market remains, right in the heart of the city and next to the new development. Both areas continue to do good business, proving that Norwich has managed to mix the best of the old and the new.

The Castle Mall shopping centre, seen from outside and inside

PART 4

Questions 21–25

- Read the text and questions below.
- For each question, mark the letter next to the correct answer – **A**, **B**, **C** or **D** –
  on your answer sheet.

When I opened the first 'Body Shop' in 1976 my only object was to earn enough
to feed my children. Today 'The Body Shop' is an international company rapidly
growing all around the world. In the years since we began I have learned a lot.
Much of what I have learned will be found in this book, for I believe that we, as a
company, have something worth saying about how to run a successful business
without giving up what we really believe in.

It's not a normal business book, nor is it just about my life. The message is that to
succeed in business you have to be different. Business can be fun, a business can
be run with love and it can do good. In business, as in life, I need to enjoy myself,
to have a feeling of family and to feel excited by the unexpected. I have always
wanted the people who work for 'The Body Shop' to feel the same way.

Now this book sends these ideas of mine out into the world, makes them public.
I'd like to think there are no limits to our 'family', no limits to what can be done.
I find that an exciting thought. I hope you do, too.

---

21 What is the writer's main purpose in writing this text?

   A   to tell the reader her life story
   B   to introduce her ideas to the reader
   C   to explain how international companies operate
   D   to tell the reader how she brought up a family

22 What would someone learn from this text?

   A   how to make a lot of money
   B   how to write a book about business
   C   what the writer's family is like
   D   what the writer's book is about

23   How does the writer feel about the business she runs?

    A   She doesn't care about success if her children are fed.
    B   She just runs it for her own entertainment.
    C   It is not like any other company.
    D   It is likely to become even more successful.

24   What kind of workers does the writer like to employ?

    A   workers who can explain her ideas
    B   workers who get on well with the public
    C   workers who have the same attitudes as she does
    D   workers who have their own families

25   What kind of person does the writer seem to be?

    A   She seems to be someone with strong opinions.
    B   She doesn't seem to be very confident.
    C   She is mainly interested in making money.
    D   She sees running a business as just a job.

PART 5

Questions 26–35

- Read the text below and choose the correct word for each space.
- For each question, mark the letter next to the correct word – **A**, **B**, **C** or **D** – **on your answer sheet**.

Example answer:

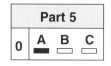

THE ROCKIES

The Rocky Mountains run almost the length **(0)** .... North America.

   They start in the North-west, but lie only a **(26)** .... hundred miles from the centre in more southern areas. Although the Rockies are smaller **(27)** .... the Alps, they are no less wonderful.

   There are many roads across the Rockies, **(28)** .... the best way to see them is to **(29)** .... by train. You start from Vancouver, **(30)** .... most attractive of Canada's big cities. Standing with its feet in the water and its head in the mountains, this city **(31)** .... its residents to ski on slopes just 15 minutes by car from the city **(32)** ....

   Thirty passenger trains a day used to **(33)** .... off from Vancouver on the cross-continent railway. Now there are just three a week, but the ride is still a great adventure. You sleep on board, **(34)** .... is fun, but travel through some of the best **(35)** .... at night.

0	**A** of	**B** down	**C** in	**D** through
26	**A** many	**B** lot	**C** few	**D** couple
27	**A** from	**B** to	**C** as	**D** than
28	**A** but	**B** because	**C** unless	**D** since
29	**A** drive	**B** travel	**C** ride	**D** pass
30	**A** a	**B** one	**C** the	**D** its
31	**A** lets	**B** allows	**C** offers	**D** gives
32	**A** centre	**B** circle	**C** middle	**D** heart
33	**A** leave	**B** get	**C** take	**D** set
34	**A** when	**B** which	**C** who	**D** where
35	**A** scenery	**B** view	**C** site	**D** beauty

WRITING

PART 1

Questions 1–5

- Here are some sentences about going to the cinema.
- For each question complete the second sentence so that it means the same as the first, **using no more than three words.**
- **Write only the missing words on your answer sheet**.

Example: Dave and Jane have been to the cinema together.

Dave .ºhas been.. **to the cinema with Jane.**

1   Nearly every seat was taken in the cinema.

There weren't .... **in the cinema.**

2   Jane had a worse seat than Dave.

Dave had .... **than Jane.**

3   Jane couldn't see the screen very well.

Jane found .... **to see the screen.**

4   Dave said that he had seen the film before.

Dave said: 'I .... **this film before.'**

5   They spent two hours watching the film.

The film .... **for two hours.**

PART 2

Question 6

You have recently moved to a town and have bought this postcard of the town to send to your penfriend.

In your postcard to your penfriend, you should

- explain why you have moved
- tell your friend what facilities the town has
- say what you dislike about living there.

Write 35–45 words on your answer sheet.

PART 3

Answer **one** of the following questions (**7** or **8**).

Question 7

- Your English teacher has asked you to write a story.
- Your story must begin with this sentence:

It was a fantastic party.

- Write your **story** in about 100 words **on your answer sheet**.

Question 8

- This is part of a letter you receive from an English friend.

> I want to find out about music in your country. Are there many live concerts? What music do you like listening to?

- Now write a letter, answering your friend's questions.
- Write your **letter** in about 100 words **on your answer sheet**.

PAPER 2   LISTENING   about 35 minutes
(including 6 minutes transfer time)

PART 1

Questions 1–7

- There are seven questions in this part.
- For each question there are three pictures and a short recording.
- Choose the correct picture and put a tick (✓) in the box below it.

Example: What's the time?

A ✓   B ☐   C ☐

1   Where is the station?

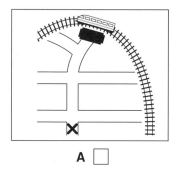 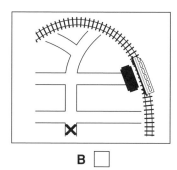 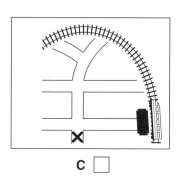

A ☐   B ☐   C ☐

2   Where did the woman put the calculator?

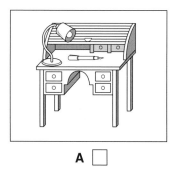 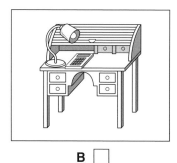 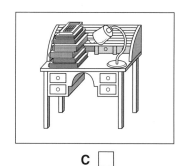

A ☐   B ☐   C ☐

3 Where is Helen?

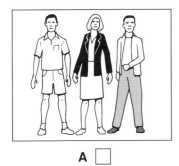

A ☐

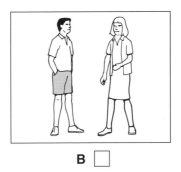

B ☐

C ☐

4 Which building was hit by lightning?

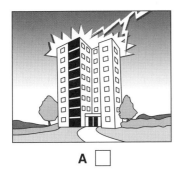

A ☐

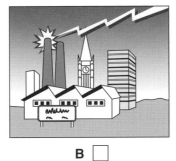

B ☐

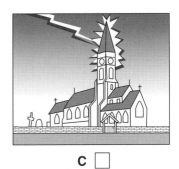

C ☐

5 What does the woman want to buy?

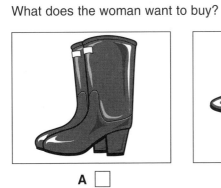

A ☐

B ☐

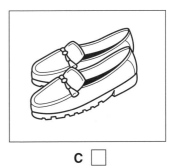

C ☐

6 Which picture does the woman decide to send?

A ☐   B ☐   C ☐

7 Which hotel has the man chosen?

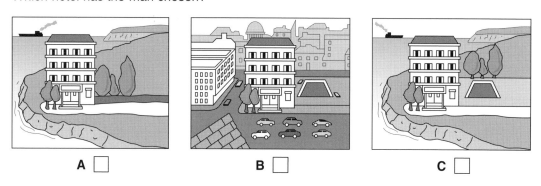

A ☐   B ☐   C ☐

PART 2

Questions 8–13

- You will hear a radio interview with a man who works on an international camp.
- For each question, put a tick (✓) in the correct box.

8   If you want to apply for the Camp you must

    A ☐ be a student.

    B ☐ be at least twenty-four years old.

    C ☐ speak more than one language.

9   In a Camp tent you can expect to

    A ☐ mix with other nationalities.

    B ☐ share with five other people.

    C ☐ know the other people.

10   The Camp want people who are

    A ☐ good at cooking.

    B ☐ good organisers.

    C ☐ able to mix well.

11   What do you have to take to the Camp?

    A ☐ a tent

    B ☐ a map

    C ☐ pictures

12   As a Camp member you should

A ☐ be a good singer.

B ☐ join in performances.

C ☐ be good at acting.

13   The Camp fees must be paid

A ☐ in dollars.

B ☐ by cheque.

C ☐ before the Camp starts.

PART 3

Questions 14–19

- You will hear a young woman who has applied for an office job talking about her jobs abroad.
- For each question, fill in the missing information in the numbered space.

INTERVIEW FORM

Name: .... *Vicky Brownlow* ....

Age: .... *22 years* ....

Position applied for: .... *Office Manager* ....

Two years' experience abroad

First job   – worked for (**14**) ....

.... – length of time stayed (**15**) ....

Second job – worked as (**16**) .... in a hotel

Third job   – worked for (**17**) ....

.... – got up at (**18**) ....

Bank International:

.... – worked in (**19**) ....

PART 4

Questions 20–25

- Look at the six sentences for this part.
- You will hear a conversation between a father and his daughter, Sonia.
- Decide if each sentence is correct or incorrect.
- If it is correct, put a tick (✓) in the box under **A** for **YES**. If it is not correct, put a tick (✓) in the box under **B** for **NO**.

		A YES	B NO
20	Sonia would like a car for her birthday.	☐	☐
21	Sonia's friend Maria has her own car.	☐	☐
22	Sonia has talked to Maria about learning to drive.	☐	☐
23	Sonia offers to get a job at weekends.	☐	☐
24	Sonia's father understands how his daughter feels.	☐	☐
25	Sonia suggests cooking a meal on her birthday.	☐	☐

Visual material for the Speaking test

1A

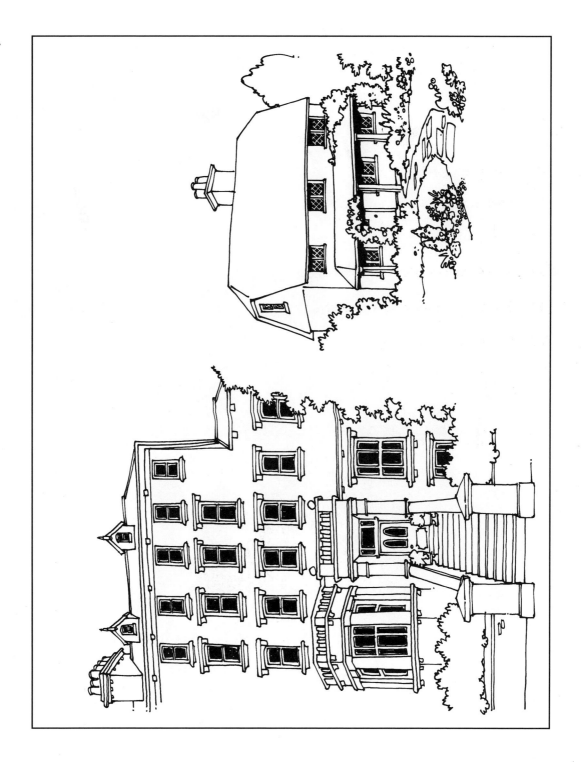

1B

2B

3B

4B

2A

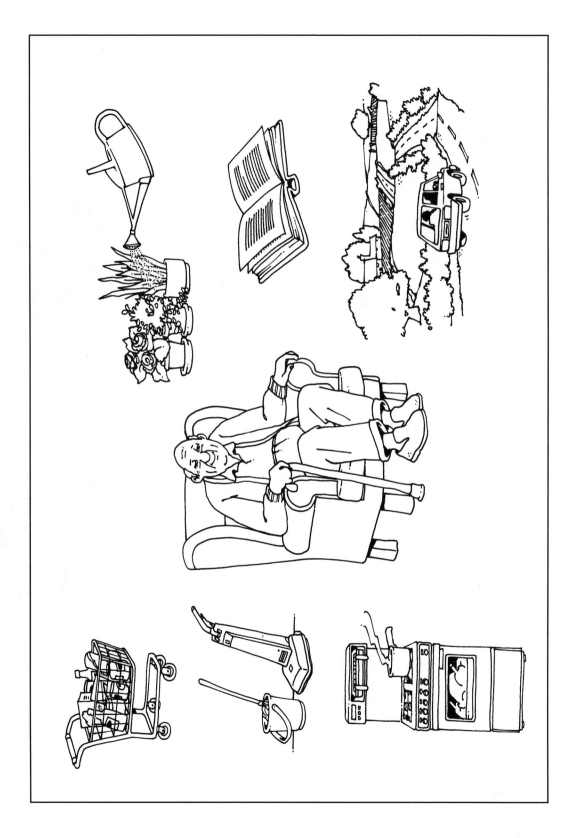

3A

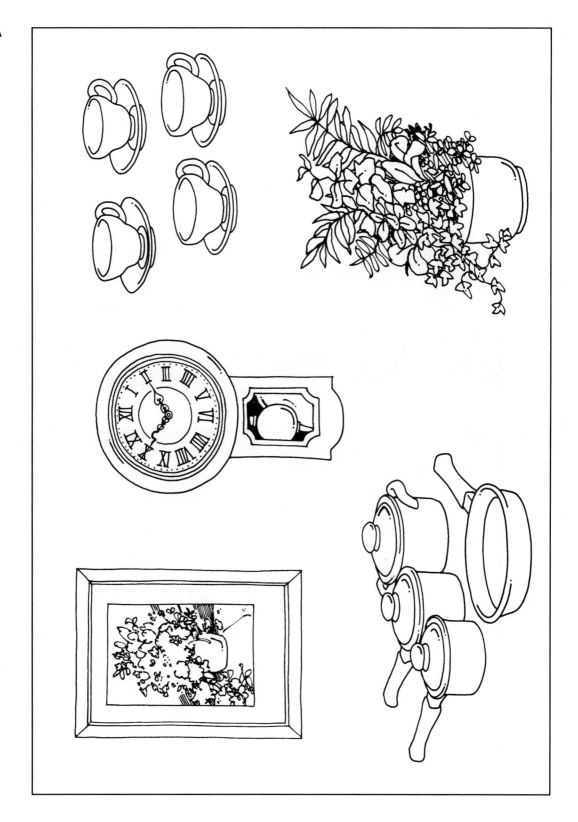

1C

2C

3C

4C

Visual material for the Speaking test

4A

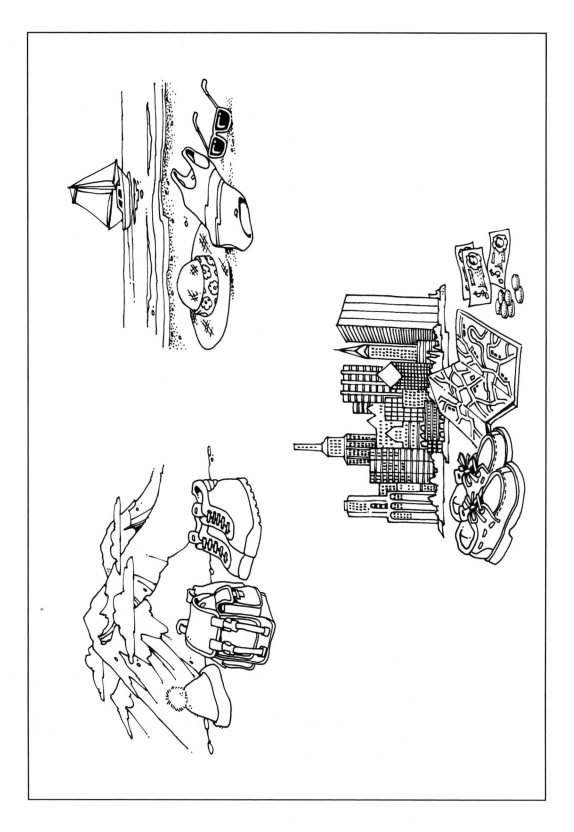

About the Speaking test

The Speaking test lasts about 10 to 12 minutes. You take the test with another candidate. There are two examiners in the room. One examiner talks to you and the other examiner listens to you. Both the examiners give you marks.

Part 1

The examiners introduce themselves and then one examiner asks you and your partner to say your names and spell them. This examiner then asks you questions about yourself, your daily life, interests, etc.

Part 2

The examiner asks you to talk about something together and gives you a drawing to help you.

Part 3

You each have a chance to talk by yourselves. The examiner gives you a colour photograph to look at and asks you to talk about it. When you have finished talking, the examiner gives your partner a different photograph to look at and to talk about.

Part 4

The examiner asks you and your partner to say more about the subject of the photographs in Part 3. You may be asked to give your opinion or to talk about something that has happened to you.

Test 4

PAPER 1 READING AND WRITING (1 hour 30 minutes)

READING

PART 1

Questions 1–5

- Look at the text in each question.
- What does it say?
- Mark the letter next to the correct explanation – **A**, **B** or **C** – **on your answer sheet**.

Example:

0

A Do not leave your bicycle touching the window.

B Do not ride your bicycle in this area.

C Broken glass may damage your bicycle tyres.

Example answer:
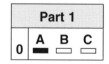

1

PARKING IN THIS
SPACE FOR DOCTOR
ON DUTY ONLY

A Tell the doctor if you need to park here.

B Only the doctor working today can park here.

C Park in this space only in an emergency.

2

To: Heidi
From: Ruth

Congratulations on the new job. Do you think they'd take me as well? Like you, I'm available until September. Could you tell them about me?

A Heidi will start her new job in September.

B Ruth wants Heidi to help her find employment.

C Ruth has offered to talk to Heidi's boss about her.

3

WARNING –
SECURITY CAMERAS IN USE AROUND THIS BUILDING

A Cameras cannot be used near this building.

B You must look after your cameras here.

C This building is guarded by cameras.

4

☎ **Message**

Helena

Ronan called from the theatre: the café opposite is closing so everyone's going down to the club early. Join them there when you can.

Where should Helena meet the others?

A at the café

B at the theatre

C at the club

5

WE HAVE MANY FLATS AVAILABLE TO RENT IN THIS AREA

A We offer a choice of flats to rent in this area.

B This is the best area to find a flat.

C Flats in this area do not cost a lot.

PART 2

Questions 6–10

- The people below all want to go on a short trip.
- On the opposite page there are descriptions of eight trips which a ferry company is offering.
- Decide which place (**letters A–H**) would be the most suitable for each person or group of people (**numbers 6–10**).
- For each of these numbers mark the correct letter **on your answer sheet**.

6   Ray and three of his friends would like to spend a whole weekend driving around in nice scenery and enjoying some of the local food.

7   Phil and Adam want to go on a comfortable trip which takes them quickly to an interesting city. Then they want to enjoy at least two days of sightseeing.

8   Mike, Kathy and their three children don't have much money, but they want a special day out this Saturday. They must be back home by 9 p.m.

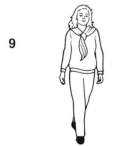

9   Kirsten is a Dutch student who is studying in Scotland. She doesn't drive, but wants a day trip to see some beautiful scenery and spend a little time by the sea.

10   Clare and Robert want to enjoy some good food, but would also like to give their two young children a day to remember. They don't mind if they spend a lot of money.

A Marine Life, France

The chance to experience the oceans of the world. Children will love the observatory, with water all around them and enormous fish swimming above their heads! Afterwards you eat at a world-famous local restaurant before boarding the ferry at 9 p.m. Not cheap, but a great day out!

B Amsterdamer

Sail out in the evening and enjoy over 12 hours in the Netherlands, returning the following night. After a good Dutch breakfast you travel by train direct to the heart of the wonderful city of Amsterdam. The sightseeing and places to shop will make this a day to remember. Weekends only.

C Ireland by Car

Once you arrive in Ireland you're quickly on beautiful country roads, with friendly villages where you can stop for a delicious bite to eat. The special price allows you to take your car and up to five people away for 48 hours, and two nights' hotel accommodation can be arranged for a little extra.

D French Hypermarket Day Trip

Whether you want to buy or just look, you'll love this tour. The enormous Darney shopping centre is a shopper's dream! You will find a great number of local goods on sale, and clothes and kitchen goods are excellent value. Free children's entertainment all day. Leaves 10:00, back at 19:00.

E Shop Till You Drop

For good value shopping, take our newest cruise-ferry and you needn't even get off! Leaving at 11 a.m., our duty-free shopping centre, more a floating department store than an on-board shop, opens at midday. We're back by 4 p.m. Sorry, only four people per ticket.

F Belgium by Hydrofoil

A four-day trip. From England you cross to Belgium in just 100 minutes by hydrofoil! You are served food and drinks during the crossing, then continue your journey to Brussels, or another beautiful city, on the fast Belgian railway network.

G A Taste of the Good Life in France

After a relaxing voyage, you visit a beautiful area which is famous for its good things to eat. There you can enjoy some sightseeing and choose from a number of wonderful restaurants. Sail back on the night crossing. Sorry, adults only!

H Sea and Mountains in Northern Ireland

Explore the Northern Ireland countryside, including the amazing Mountains of Mourne and the small seaside holiday town of Newcastle. The ferry leaves the port in Scotland at 7:30 and arrives back at 22:20. Transport in Northern Ireland is by air-conditioned coach.

PART 3

Questions 11–20

- Look at the sentences below about Nene Valley Railway.
- Read the text on the opposite page to decide if each sentence is correct or incorrect.
- If it is correct, mark **A on your answer sheet**.
- If it is not correct, mark **B on your answer sheet**.

11   Nene Valley Railway carries goods between distant cities.

12   One adult and three children can buy a Family Fare.

13   The Railway is the only attraction in Nene Park.

14   The biggest steam engine at Wansford is French.

15   You can see the German engine only at certain times of the year.

16   Passengers must pay extra to see the train collection at Wansford.

17   The Railway has appeared in at least one film.

18   Groups of school children can only visit the railway in May or June.

19   A group of fifty pupils pays more per child than a group of sixty.

20   You can book a train for a private party.

NENE VALLEY RAILWAY

About the Railway

The twelve kilometre-long Nene Valley Railway passes through the lovely Nene Park, from an Eastern terminus at Peterborough to the Railway's headquarters at Wansford (next to the A1 main road). A two-kilometre extension of the Railway takes passengers through Wansford Tunnel to the quiet beauty of Yarwell, the present Western end of the line.

Fares: adult £10.00, child £5.00, Family Fare (up to 2 adults and 3 children) £25.00. Special prices may apply on public holidays.

Nene Park

With golf courses and a large Caravan Club site, why not make it a complete day out for the family by visiting Nene Park? There are thousands of hectares of public parkland with boating lakes, picnic areas and a nature reserve, as well as a miniature railway.

Wansford

Wansford Station is the home of a unique collection of historic trains from many parts of Europe. This includes such famous types as the elegant *De Glen Compound* locomotive from France, and the German Class 52 *Kriegslok* (the largest working steam engine in Britain) as well as '92 Squadron' and 'Mayflower' which were built in Britain. You can see these engines all year round whether or not the Nene Valley Railway is running.

The buffet, bar and souvenir shop, however, are only open on days when the train is running. A site entrance fee of £2.00 for adults and £1.00 for children is charged at Wansford.

A Famous Railway

Nene Valley Railway is a favourite with film makers, due in particular to its ability to take on the appearance of a railway in any part of Europe. *Octopussy*, in the series of James Bond movies, is a good example of what can be done. Come and see where it was filmed.

Services for Schools

The Railway runs special timetable services from May to July to allow school groups to visit the railway and for teachers to set projects. The work can be done while pupils are here or in the classroom. A special educational pack is available, price £1.50 plus postage. At other times of the year, school parties can hire the train ('Teddy Bear') with up to 3 carriages to travel along the Railway on non-service days. One month's prior booking is requested. There are special low fares for groups of 60 or more pupils. Telephone 01780 784444 for further information.

Private Hire of Trains

The Railway is a popular place for special family occasions or a company visit. It can provide the setting for a most interesting afternoon or evening out. Special programmes can be arranged to meet your wishes to include buffet, bar, entertainment, discos, etc. For further information please contact the General Manager at Wansford Station.

PART 4

Questions 21–25

- Read the text and questions below.
- For each question, mark the letter next to the correct answer – **A**, **B**, **C** or **D** –
  on your answer sheet.

Some people have complained about this year's collection, *New Writing 3*,
although I cannot understand why. Surely 500 pages of original writing of this
quality, for £6.99, is pretty amazing?

Fiction – both parts of novels and complete short stories – makes up most of the
book. There are some enjoyable pieces by famous writers, such as Candia
McWilliam and Rose Tremain. It's a strange fact that the less well-known people
seem to have written mainly about food. Take my advice about Jane Harris's
Those Nails – this piece should definitely not be read just after meals. It contains
some very unpleasant scenes which could turn your stomach!

There is fine work from nineteen poets, including R. S. Thomas and John
Burnside. There are pieces from novels-in-progress by Jim Crace and Jane Rogers.
Finally, there is a little non-fiction, which includes a very funny article by Alan
Rusbridger on certain newspapers, and an extraordinary piece about herself from
Ursula Owen. This is an exceptional collection and I for one can't wait to see what
next year's choice will include.

---

21   What is the writer trying to do in the text?

    A   give her opinions about a new book
    B   give some information about new writers
    C   give some advice to writers
    D   give her opinion of newspaper journalists

22   Why would somebody read the text?

    A   to find out more details about something
    B   to learn what next year's collection will contain
    C   to find out about Alan Rusbridger's new novel
    D   to decide whether to complain about something

23 What does the writer think of *New Writing 3*?

   A It's too long.
   B It's very amusing.
   C It's very good.
   D It's too serious.

24 How might you feel after reading Jane Harris's piece?

   A hungry
   B excited
   C unhappy
   D sick

25 Which of the following describes *New Writing 3*?

A
Great value:
two novels, poems and
articles for only £6.99

B
Great value:
the best of new writing for
only £6.99

C
Great value:
poems by Tremain,
Harris and Burnside for
only £6.99

D
Great value:
newspapers for a whole
year for only £6.99

PART 5

Questions 26–35

- Read the text below and choose the correct word for each space.
- For each question, mark the letter next to the correct word – **A**, **B**, **C** or **D** –
  on your answer sheet.

Example answer:

Part 5			
0	A ■	B ☐	C ☐	D ☐

CARTOON FILMS

Cartoon films have very **(0)** .... limits. If you can draw something, you can
(26) .... it move on the cinema screen. The use **(27)** .... new ideas and
advanced computer programs means that cartoons are becoming exciting again for
people of **(28)** .... ages.

By the **(29)** .... of the 1970s, the cinema world had decided that cartoons were
only for children.

But soon **(30)** .... , one or two directors had some original new ideas. They
proved that it was possible to make films in which both adults and children could
(31) .... the fun.

However, not **(32)** .... cartoon film was successful. *The Black Cauldron*, for
example, failed, mainly because it was too **(33)** .... for children and too childish
for adults. Directors learnt from this **(34)** .... , and the film companies began to
make large **(35)** .... of money again.

0	**A** few	**B** any	**C** little	**D** much
26	**A** get	**B** cause	**C** wish	**D** make
27	**A** for	**B** of	**C** with	**D** by
28	**A** more	**B** other	**C** all	**D** these
29	**A** end	**B** finish	**C** departure	**D** back
30	**A** afterwards	**B** later	**C** next	**D** then
31	**A** divide	**B** add	**C** mix	**D** share
32	**A** every	**B** both	**C** any	**D** each
33	**A** nervous	**B** fearful	**C** afraid	**D** frightening
34	**A** damage	**B** crime	**C** mistake	**D** fault
35	**A** amounts	**B** accounts	**C** numbers	**D** totals

WRITING

PART 1

Questions 1–5

- Here are some sentences about visiting a hospital.
- For each question complete the second sentence so that it means the same as the first, **using no more than three words**.
- **Write only the missing words on your answer sheet**.

Example: The nurses' home is behind the hospital.

The hospital is .in front of. **the nurses' home.**

1 My appointment with Dr Gibson is at ten o'clock.

At ten o'clock I am .... **an appointment with Dr Gibson.**

2 The office is Dr Gibson's.

This office .... **to Dr Gibson.**

3 Dr Gibson told me to take off my shoes and socks.

Dr Gibson said: 'Please take .... **and socks off.'**

4 'It would be a good idea to take more exercise.'

'You really .... **to take more exercise.'**

5 I was given some information about a local gym.

The hospital .... **some information about a local gym.**

PART 2

Question 6

You have received some good news and want to tell your friend in Australia about it.

Write an e-mail to your friend. In your e-mail, you should

- explain your good news
- say how you feel about it
- ask about your friend's family.

Write 35–45 words on your answer sheet.

PART 3

Answer **one** of the following questions (**7** or **8**).

Question 7

- This is part of a letter you receive from your penfriend.

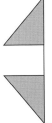

> I'm glad you like learning English. Your teacher sounds really nice – and your friends do too! Tell me all about your English classes.

- Now write a letter to your penfriend.
- Write your **letter** in about 100 words **on your answer sheet**.

Question 8

- You have to write a story for your English teacher.
- Your story must have this title:

A broken window

- Write your **story** in about 100 words **on your answer sheet**.

PAPER 2   LISTENING   about 35 minutes
(including 6 minutes transfer time)

PART 1

Questions 1–7

- There are seven questions in this part.
- For each question there are three pictures and a short recording.
- Choose the correct picture and put a tick (✓) in the box below it.

Example: What's the time?

A ✓   B ☐   C ☐

1   Where are the woman's glasses?

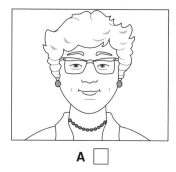 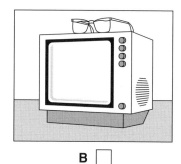 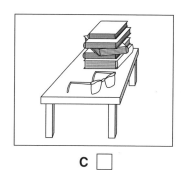

A ☐   B ☐   C ☐

2   What damage was done to the car?

A ☐   B ☐   C ☐

3 What did she bring?

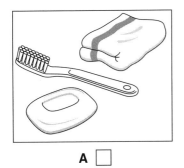 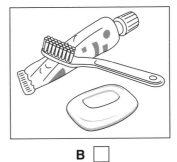 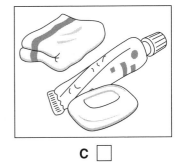

A ☐ B ☐ C ☐

4 What did Sally buy?

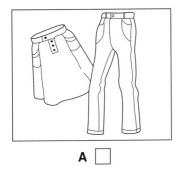 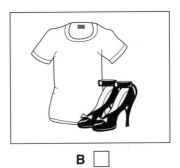 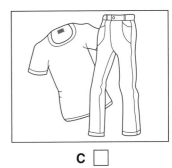

A ☐ B ☐ C ☐

5 Where are the man and his grandma?

A ☐ B ☐ C ☐

6 What would John like to be?

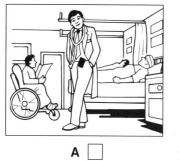 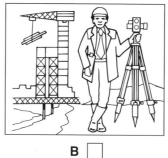 

A ☐ B ☐ C ☐

7 Which pianist are the two people talking about?

A ☐ B ☐ C ☐

PART 2

Questions 8–13

- You will hear a talk given to visitors to a fashion museum.
- For each question, put a tick (✓) in the correct box.

8   The speaker says that fashion now interests   A ☐ rich people.

B ☐ young people.

C ☐ most people.

9   Fashion clothes which were made before   A ☐ individually made.
     the 1900s were

B ☐ copied from pictures.

C ☐ made of light material.

10   Coco Chanel   A ☐ was born in 1908.

B ☐ changed people's ideas about fashion.

C ☐ liked wearing tight-fitting clothes.

11   In the 1920s   A ☐ white skirts were fashionable.

B ☐ clothes started to cost less.

C ☐ women took up sports.

12 Which of these was part of the 'New Look'?   **A** ☐ material with flowers

B ☐ very short skirts

C ☐ longer skirts

13 The speaker is introducing an exhibition of   **A** ☐ clothes that are very old.

B ☐ fashion for the future.

C ☐ pictures of today's fashions.

PART 3

Questions 14–19

- You will hear a man talking about Tanya Perry's life.
- For each question, fill in the missing information in the numbered space.

TANYA PERRY

Born in London in 1948.

In 1952 family moved to (**14**) ....

At school with ....*Jack Peters*.... , the famous (**15**) ....

Wrote some (**16**) .... while still at school.

During the early 1970s worked as a (**17**) ....

The film called (**18**) .... won a prize at a

French Film Festival.

Now has (**19**) .... plays in print.

PART 4

Questions 20–25

- Look at the six sentences for this part.
- You will hear a conversation between a man and a woman at home.
- Decide if each sentence is correct or incorrect.
- If it is correct, put a tick (✓) in the box under **A** for **YES**. If it is not correct, put a tick (✓) in the box under **B** for **NO**.

		A YES	B NO
20	The man wants to spend the evening at home.	☐	☐
21	The woman suggests they hire a video.	☐	☐
22	They both want to see something light.	☐	☐
23	The woman only likes to see a film once.	☐	☐
24	In the end they decide to watch a video.	☐	☐
25	The man offers to prepare some food.	☐	☐

About the Speaking test

The Speaking test lasts about 10 to 12 minutes. You take the test with another candidate. There are two examiners in the room. One examiner talks to you and the other examiner listens to you. Both the examiners give you marks.

Part 1

The examiners introduce themselves and then one examiner asks you and your partner to say your names and spell them. This examiner then asks you questions about yourself, your daily life, interests, etc.

Part 2

The examiner asks you to talk about something together and gives you a drawing to help you.

Part 3

You each have a chance to talk by yourselves. The examiner gives you a colour photograph to look at and asks you to talk about it. When you have finished talking, the examiner gives your partner a different photograph to look at and to talk about.

Part 4

The examiner asks you and your partner to say more about the subject of the photographs in Part 3. You may be asked to give your opinion or to talk about something that has happened to you.

Key

Test 1

PAPER 1   READING AND WRITING

READING

Part 1

1 C   2 B   3 B   4 A   5 C

Part 2

6 C   7 F   8 G   9 D   10 B

Part 3

11 B   12 A   13 B   14 A   15 A   16 B   17 B
18 B   19 A   20 B

Part 4

21 D   22 C   23 A   24 C   25 B

Part 5

26 B   27 B   28 C   29 A   30 C   31 B   32 C
33 D   34 A   35 A

WRITING

Part 1

1 My parents prefer jazz to classical music.

My parents think jazz	is better	**than classical music.**

2 My parents only go swimming at the weekend.

On weekdays, my parents aren't	able to	**go swimming.**

3 If I finish my homework, I can go out at the weekend.

I can't go out at the weekend	unless	**I finish my homework.**

4 My sister watches more TV than me.

I don't	watch	TV	as/so much/often as	my sister does.

5 My parents suggested going out for a meal.

My parents said, 'Why	don't	we go out for a meal?'

Part 2

Task-specific Mark scheme

The content elements that need to be covered are:

i   an apology
ii an explanation for the delay
iii a suggestion for when Jo could come in the future.

The following sample answers can be used as a guide when marking.

SAMPLE A (Test 1, Question 6: Card to Jo)

> Dear Jo
> As you know, the other day I invited you next month.
> I'm sorry but I have to delay it because there is may
> friend's wedding party that day.
> Could you come here on 22th of October.
> Yours sincerely
> Kyoko

Examiner Comments

This is a very good answer. All three content elements are covered appropriately and within the word limit. Language errors are present, but they are minor and do not affect the message being clearly communicated to the reader.

Band: 5

SAMPLE B (Test 1, Question 6: Card to Jo)

Dear Jo

First of all, I apologise to you for delay to visit. I have to go to library next month, because I have some exams. So, I must study for exam at daytime with my class mate.

But in the night time, I'll be free for you.

I suggest that you come to my house and stay with me.

When would you be convenient to come?

I'll happy to you're comming.

See you later

Examiner Comments

In this script, all three content elements are attempted but the third one (suggest when it would be convenient for Jo to come) has been inadequately dealt with – the candidate does include a general comment that night-time is when he'll be free, but then asks Jo, rather than suggesting when it would be convenient. The message also requires some effort by the reader, due to the language errors.

Band: 3

SAMPLE C (Test 1, Question 6: Card to Jo)

> Hi Jo!
>
> How are you? I hope you are fine. I'm fine, but I miss you so much. I think if I see you again, I'll be much happy.
>
> Next month I'm not working, and my parents going to holiday. So I'll be alone! I have lots of plan for next month, If you can come my house.
>
> Before come, please send me your flyt delayes, because I'll collect to you at airport.
>
> I'm waiting your repley.
>
> I'm forward seeing you again.
>
> Love, Gamze

Examiner Comments

This is a poor attempt, with little relevance to the task set. It appears that the initial rubric has been disregarded or misunderstood, as the content is about Jo visiting next month. Similarly, the first two bullet points have been ignored. The answer is also much too long at around 90 words, failing to demonstrate the ability to write a short message.

Band: 1

Part 3

The following sample answers can be used as a guide when marking.

SAMPLE D (Test 1, Question 7: 'Carla looked at the car in surprise')

Carla looked at the car in surprise. She said "Oh my God! that car is wonderful".

Her father promised her a car like that, but he forgot it, at least she told me it.

Carla is too young to drive a car, I think that her father should wait some years to give her a car, but she make up her mind and asked her father every day "where the car is, I want it", you promised for me".

Now her father want that I try to change her mind, because he think is too dangeous for her.

I said I will try, but I don't promis that I will be able to do it.

Examiner Comments

This answer is ambitious, but flawed by a number of mostly non-impeding errors in, for example, tenses, subject-verb agreement, question formation and spelling. The story is well organised and the range of structures and vocabulary used is more than adequate. With fewer errors, the script would have been placed in Band 4.

Band: 3

SAMPLE E (Test 1, Question 7: 'Carla looked at the car in surprise')

Carla looked at the car in surprise.

When the driver noticed her, it was so late. She woke up at the driver's house in two or three hours. She asked him why he hadn't called an ambalance, but soon she found the answer before he explaines because he looks so young. She could guess that he had been driving without the license.

They talked each other about themselves. They fell in love by the time she leaves his house. They made a promise to see again before saying good-bye.

Examiner Comments

This is a good attempt, requiring only a little effort by the reader. The writing is ambitious, and reasonably well organised, although would benefit from more linking of sentences. There is evidence of a wide range of structures, including the past perfect continuous tense and good use of pronouns. A range of vocabulary is attempted, though spelling is not always accurate.

Band: 4

SAMPLE F (Test 1, Question 7: 'Carla looked at the car in surprise')

> Carla looked at the car in surprise. Because there were too many people. Almost 12 people was in the car. Carla said that how they could do. And A few minute later, a big man drived the car slow. And then he suddenly stoped the car and shouted to people in the car that whe we didn't walk Because of his shouting, some people walked and another people went by the car, at last. All in the street laught.

Examiner Comments

The story requires some effort by the reader, mainly due to flawed sentence structure and a number of errors, some of which impede communication, for example, *Carla said that how they could do.* However, the range used is adequate to the task, so this answer would be placed at the top of Band 2.

Band: 2

SAMPLE G (Test 1, Question 8: 'The last film I saw')

> The last film I saw is "Austin Powers in Gold Member". It was absolutely fantastic!!
> I've seen "Austin Powers 2". It was great too. But "Austin Powers 3" is greatest than
> "2". It was in Tom Cruse, Kevin Spacy and so on. Also it was in Tokyo. It was so
> strange. For example, Mt. Fuji isn't in Tokyo. But in the film, it was in Tokyo. How
> funny! Of course, I know you don't know about Japan very much, But it is still
> interesting, I think. As if you haven't seen "Austin Powers 1 and 2", you will enjoy
> this film. Because I want to see it again! I recommed it to you. You should see it.

Examiner Comments

This is an adequate attempt at the task, despite the absence of opening and closing
letter formulae. The letter is reasonably well organised, with some linking of sentences.
The range of structures and vocabulary used is adequate and all errors are non-
impeding.

Band: 3

SAMPLE H (Test 1, Question 8: 'The last film I saw')

Hi, mate!!

How's it going? I was very busy this week. But. You know that I love films. I saw the film with the name of 'Bend it like Beckham' It's a very interesting film about football. An indian girl who wanted to play football was the main story. Her parents don't let her play. But she's a very good football player, she's better than a boy who doesn't know how to play football. Finally, she went to America for proffesional league. Santa Barbara. I'm not sure of the team name. Anyway, it's a happy ending for her and for her family.

I recomended the film to Mike and Mike saw the film. He loved it. So I do recomend to you the film 'Bend it like Beckham'.

If I were you, I'd go the cinema right now. Have a good weekend. See you soon.

Bye.

Examiner Comments

This is a very good answer, showing confident and ambitious use of language. The letter is well organised, with good linking of sentences. There is a wide range of structures, including *If I were you, I'd ...* and vocabulary, as well as appropriate expressions, for example *happy ending*. Errors are minor and mainly due to ambition.

Band: 5

SAMPLE I (Test 1, Question 8: 'The last film I saw')

Hello dear Maria,
In your last letter you asked me to write to you about the last film which I've seen. It was „Gladiator" It's a very interesting film with Russel Crow I love this actor, you knew that. But is not only because of him. I also love to watch histori films.

Examiner Comments

This is an inadequate attempt at the task, due to its length (the answer appears unfinished and is only 50 words long). There is some evidence of range in the language used and the task has been addressed.

Band: 2

PAPER 2   LISTENING

Part 1

1 C   2 A   3 A   4 B   5 C   6 A   7 C

Part 2

8 C   9 B   10 B   11 A   12 B   13 C

Part 3

(*Recognisable spelling accepted in all except number 18*)

14 science
15 running
16 bicycle/bike
17 (he) helps (his uncle) to milk (fifty) cows
      (he) helps (to) do the milking
      (he) sometimes cleans (the) cowsheds
      (he) milks (his uncle's) cows
      helps his uncle (on his farm)
      works at/on (his) uncle's farm
      (he) helps to look after/looks after (his) uncle's cows
18 Monday(s)
19 farmer/have (his) own farm
      work in (the) countryside

Part 4

20 A   21 B   22 B   23 A   24 B   25 A

Test 1 transcript

> This is the Cambridge Preliminary English Test number 1. There are four parts to the test. You will hear each part twice.
>
> For each part of the test, there will be time for you to look through the questions and time for you to check your answers.
>
> Write your answers on the question paper. You will have six minutes at the end of the test to copy your answers on to the answer sheet.
>
> The recording will now be stopped. Please ask any questions now because you must not speak during the test.
>
> [pause]

PART 1   *Now open your question paper and look at Part 1.*

> There are seven questions in this part. For each question there are three pictures and a short recording. Choose the correct picture and put a tick in the box below it.

Before we start, here is an example.

What's the time?

Woman: Have you got the time?

Man: Yes, it's twenty past three.

[pause]

The first picture is correct so there is a tick in box A.

Look at the three pictures for question 1 now.

[pause]

Now we are ready to start. Listen carefully. You will hear each recording twice.

One. Where will the girls meet?

Girl 1: Will you meet me in the park?

Girl 2: OK. Where? By the entrance?

Girl 1: No, at the ice-cream kiosk. You know, the one by the lake.

Girl 2: OK.

[pause]

Now listen again.

[The recording is repeated.]

[pause]

Two. Which chair does the man want?

Man: Good afternoon. Can you show me your office chairs? I'm looking for
           something with a high back and arms.

[pause]

Now listen again.

[The recording is repeated.]

[pause]

Three. Which picture shows what the girls need?

Girl 1: Now, have we got everything? Flour, butter, a lemon, milk …

Girl 2: Don't we need eggs?

Girl 1: Of course! Two eggs.

[pause]

Now listen again.

[The recording is repeated.]

[pause]

Four. Which picture shows what happened?

Woman: Look at that mirror – how did it get broken?

Boy: We were playing ball and I missed it.

Woman: I've told you before you are not to play ball in the house. Well, you will
              both have to buy a new mirror.

[pause]

Now listen again.

[The recording is repeated.]

[pause]

Five. What is Sarah's mother doing?

Sarah: When can we go out, Mum?
Mother: In about half an hour, Sarah, when I've finished doing the
         washing-up.

[pause]

Now listen again.

[The recording is repeated.]

[pause]

Six. What luggage is the man taking on holiday?

Woman: I thought you were only taking two suitcases on holiday with you?
Man: Well, I was, but I decided to take my overnight bag as well. I couldn't
         get everything into two cases and there's no way I could carry a third!

[pause]

Now listen again.

[The recording is repeated.]

[pause]

Seven. Which photograph does the man like?

Man: I'm really disappointed with my holiday photos. The only good one is the
      one of us all standing together on the clifftop looking down at the beach.

[pause]

Now listen again.

[The recording is repeated.]

[pause]

That is the end of Part 1.

[pause]

PART 2   *Now turn to Part 2, questions 8–13.*

You will hear part of a radio programme about classical music.

*For each question, put a tick in the correct box. You now have 45 seconds to
look at the questions for Part 2.*

[pause]

Now we are ready to start. Listen carefully. You will hear the recording twice.

Presenter: … and now if you're a regular listener to this programme, you'll know
             that it's time for our weekly competition. Last week's prize of two
             theatre tickets was won by Bill Martins. Congratulations, Bill. I hope
             you've received your tickets by now.
                 This week we're offering a classical CD to the first listener who

can name the piece of music *and* the person who wrote it. I'm going to play the piece in a few minutes, but before I do, you need to get a pencil and a piece of paper, as I'm going to give you some help which should make your job a little easier. Are you ready? Right. Now, listen carefully, as you might be this week's lucky winner.

Although the person who wrote this piece of classical music was born in Italy, his parents were French and he spent most of his life in Spain. Have you got that? On to the second point: there is also a famous play which has the same title as this music and which is usually performed in the open air – in the summer. Any idea yet? I should warn you that it's not that easy.

Anyway for the next point. When this piece of music was first performed, many people in the audience got up and walked out. At the end they say there was complete silence, which I'm sure wasn't very pleasant for the writer. People thought the music was terrible and complained about wasting their money. It's amazing really, when you think how popular it is today.

And now for the last point. Part of this music has been used for an advertisement which you can see on television. I'm sure when you hear the music, you'll know what the advertisement is for. I'm not going to tell you what product it advertises, as that would almost certainly give you the answer! You can also see the advert in a lot of magazines and I think from next month this advert will also be on your cinema screens.

So that's four things to remember. And the phone number to ring if you can give us the title of the music *and* the name of the man who wrote it is 0018 937 224. And the piece of music is coming up now …

[pause]

Now listen again.

[The recording is repeated.]

That is the end of Part 2.

[pause]

PART 3   *Now turn to Part 3, questions 14–19.*

You will hear a radio programme in which young people from different parts of the country are interviewed.

For each question, fill in the missing information in the numbered space.

You now have 20 seconds to look at Part 3.

[pause]

Now we are ready to start. Listen carefully. You will hear the recording twice.

Man: Hello and welcome to our series about young people living in different parts of the country. Today you'll hear Mike Davis, who lives in Hereford, telling you something about his life.

Boy: Hello. I'm 13 years old and I go to Stanley School. I'm in Form 3, and I'm really interested in science but I find maths and especially English a bit hard. I'm good at running and I've run for the school team in the 800 metres.

Key

My dad sells farm machinery. We live in the country about four miles from school, so I get to school by bicycle. My uncle has a farm and I spend most of my free time helping out there. He's got 50 cows and I like to help him with them. I help to do the milking every Saturday and sometimes I have to clean the cowshed. It's hard work, but it's good to see everything looking clean. I painted it white last summer – I'm good at painting. My uncle's got a tractor and he says I can drive it when I'm 15. I'm looking forward to that.

On Mondays I go to the Young Farmers' Group which I've belonged to since I was 10. It's mostly fun but we also learn things, like how to look after animals properly.

I definitely want to work in the countryside when I leave school. I wouldn't like to live in a town or sit in an office all day. My father thinks I should work in his business, but I want to be like my uncle and have my own farm one day. My mother says I'll have to go to agricultural college first, so I'm going to work hard to pass all my exams.

Man: Thank you, Mike, …

[pause]

Now listen again.

[The recording is repeated.]

That is the end of Part 3.

[pause]

PART 4   *Now turn to Part 4, questions 20–25.*

Look at the six sentences for this part. You will hear a conversation between a boy, Jim, and his mother.

Decide if each sentence is correct or incorrect. If it is correct, put a tick in the box under A for YES. If it is not correct, put a tick in the box under B for NO.

You now have 20 seconds to look at the questions for Part 4.

[pause]

Now we are ready to start. Listen carefully. You will hear the recording twice.

Jim: Mum, my old bicycle needs to be repaired again.
Mother: Well then, why don't you think of buying a new one, Jim?
Jim: You know, I'd really like to buy one of those mountain bikes.
Mother: Well, what's stopping you?
Jim: Do you know how much they cost? At least £300. Where can I find that kind of money?
Mother: You could save the money. If you saved £5 a week, you would have the money you need in, let me see … just over a year.
Jim: Just over a year! But I want a new bike now. It's something I really need. I mean, I use my bike to go to college every day.
Mother: But what's so special about a mountain bike? Why do you have to have one of those? There aren't any mountains around here. Isn't an ordinary bike cheaper?
Jim: Yes. But mountain bikes are stronger, and they're better at going up hills.

Mother: We don't even have any hills near us. How much does an ordinary bike cost?

Jim: I don't know … Oh, I suppose you can get quite a good one for about £150.

Mother: Well, that sounds more reasonable. If you save £5 a week, you'll have enough money in about six months.

Jim: That won't help me get to college next term!

Mother: I really think you should learn to save some money. I'll tell you what I'll do. If you manage to save £100, I'll give you the rest. That way you'll be riding a new bike in a few months. Go and get the old one repaired, and bring the bill to me.

Jim: Thanks, Mum. I suppose I'll just have to ride my old bike for a little longer. I must say I had hoped to be able to get a new one straight away. It's going to take me ages to save up. I wish …

[pause]

Now listen again.

[The recording is repeated.]

That is the end of Part 4.

[pause]

You now have six minutes to check and copy your answers on to the answer sheet.

Note: Teacher, stop the tape here and time six minutes. Remind students when there is **one** minute remaining.

[pause]

That is the end of the test.

Test 2

PAPER 1   READING AND WRITING

READING

Part 1

1 A   2 B   3 C   4 C   5 B

Part 2

6 D   7 G   8 F   9 B   10 C

Part 3

11 A	12 A	13 B	14 B	15 B	16 A	17 B	18 A
19 B	20 B						

Part 4

21 D   22 C   23 B   24 A   25 A

Part 5

26 A	27 A	28 D	29 D	30 A	31 C	32 B	33 B
34 C	35 B						

WRITING

Part 1

1 When she has to walk to the supermarket she finds it tiring.

She gets	tired	**when she has to walk to the supermarket.**

2 She is often driven to the supermarket by her neighbour.

Her neighbour often	gives her	**a lift to the supermarket.**

3 There are many types of coffee there.

You can buy a	lot of/variety/range of	**types of coffee there.**

4 She asked an assistant how much the Colombian coffee cost.

She asked: 'How	much does	**the Colombian coffee cost?'**

5 The Colombian coffee cost less than the Kenyan coffee.

The Colombian coffee wasn't	as/so expensive/dear	**as the Kenyan coffee.**

Part 2

Task-specific Mark scheme

The e-mail should incorporate the following points:

i   expression of thanks for stay
ii what was most enjoyable about the countryside
iii suggestion for where to meet next time.

The following sample answers can be used as a guide when marking.

SAMPLE A (Test 2, Question 6: e-mail to friends)

> Hi,
> Thank you for nice days with you. I most enjoyed to swim in the nice sea. So if you have a time, I'd like to see you again. Shall we go to France next time?
> Love Tomoko

Examiner Comments

All three content elements are adequately dealt with, within the word limit. However, the reference to swimming in the sea is not appropriate to the 'countryside' specified in the rubric and second bullet point (though this may be a language error, for 'lake'). On the whole, the message is communicated successfully. It is not necessary for candidates to include the format details of an e-mail.

Band: 4

Key

SAMPLE B (Test 2, Question 6: e-mail to friends)

> Hello! How's it going? I'm fine. I could enjoy when I went to the countryside with you because there were a lot of nature. I couldn't see them when I lived in Japan. I thought I wanted to go there again. Shall we meet again, if possible? I'm looking forward to meeting you. See you!! Bye!! Shin

Examiner Comments

In this script, only the second content element has been adequately dealt with. Although the candidate sounds enthusiastic ('I could enjoy'), this does not amount to thanking the friends. With regard to the third point, the candidate suggests meeting again, but doesn't mention where. Two content elements are therefore unsuccessfully dealt with.

Band: 2

SAMPLE C (Test 2, Question 6: e-mail to friends)

Dear Mary and Fred

Are you already missing me? I'm very well. the travel back was good.
I really loved that peacefull place. I'm so thankfull for all and I'd like to offer you a dinner in my home next saturday. What do you think?

See you
Leticia

Examiner Comments

This is a very good attempt, covering all content elements appropriately. Although language errors are present, they do not affect the clarity of the message, which would have a positive effect on Mary and Fred.

Band: 5

Key

Part 3

The following sample answers can be used as a guide when marking.

SAMPLE D (Test 2, Question 7: Letter to a penfriend)

Dear John,

The first and most important issue is not to reduce the food you eat dayly. You can change the menu and the way you eat but if you start a diet by yourself the first thing you'll lose is your health.

You can find many good gyms and if you want I can send the names for you in another letter. However, you don't need necessarily to go to a gym to stay fit. Some small changes to your life can do a big difference. For example, you can start by walking some time during the morning or in the lunch time.

I hope you don't have any health problem and it would be nice if you went to a doctor for a check-up before starting any exercise.

Best regards,

Fabio

Examiner Comments

This is a very good attempt, showing confident use of language in an appropriate letter of advice. The range of structures and vocabulary used is wide and occasionally above PET level. Errors are minor, due to ambition and all non-impeding, for example *do a big difference*. The letter reads very naturally.

Band: 5

SAMPLE E (Test 2, Question 7: Letter to a penfriend)

Hi, Lena

I'm so happy receive letter from you.

You asked me some advice? What can I tell you? If you want to be healthy all your live, try avoid tea, coffee, alcohol. Give up smoking, give up go to night clabs every friday and saturday. Take cold shower every day, 2 times per day – it will be better. Don't eat any sold and pepper food. Don't forgot about sport. Swimming (I think) – it is the best of all for your body and soul. If you don't like water you can go to a gim or choose for you fitness-programme. Common, try it.

But this are just advices. A part of them ban live happy. We need change our life-stily for it. Sometime it is very boring.

Good luck. Be strong girl and maybe by next year I will have seen your result.

Miss you, my darling.

Examiner Comments

This answer is ambitious but flawed by a high number of errors, some of which are quite basic, for example, *Don't forgot about sport*. As a letter, it flows and contains some excellent touches, for example the encouragement at the close, *Be strong girl ...* There is evidence of a range of vocabulary, for example, *body and soul*. It is also quite well organised and would have been in a higher band, had the accuracy been better.

Band: 3

SAMPLE F (Test 2, Question 7: Letter to a penfriend)

Dear Emma,

It's an easy way to keep fit and healthy.

Firstly, you must avoid all fat and junk foods. I know you really like Double Cheese Burger but it make a lot of bad effects to your health.

Secondly, you will try to eat fruits and vegetables because it's plenty of vitamins, the good sources of good health.

Thirdly, stop to smoke now. I know it's very hard for you to avoid it but I'm sure that you can do anything you want.

Finally, Go out! Swimming, jogging and going to Fitness club will help you keep in shape. I'm absolutely sure that if you can do everything above you will have a good heath and shape too.

Let's go!

take care,
Moou

Examiner Comments

This is a good attempt, showing fairly ambitious use of language and a more than adequate range of vocabulary, including nouns and expressions relevant to the topic, for example *junk foods, vitamins, keep in shape*. It is well organised and linked, requiring no effort by the reader. There are, however, some non-impeding errors.

Band: 4

SAMPLE G **(Test 2, Question 8: 'An exciting adventure')**

Once upon a time a monkey live on a big tree near a river. He was a clever monkey. He wants to go on the other side of river to see how the other animals live there and if they have a better food.

He didn't know how to get to the other side of the river, expecialy because in the river was a lot of crocodiles.

One day he decided that he will build a boat of wooden plates.

He get a wooden plates and some kind of cotton wool, so He made a boat. He put it into the water, but when he came on the middle of the river the boat crash down. He must to swim and the crocodiles was there. He swim on the other side of river very fast and crocodiles didn't eat him, but now he wasn't at home, he was on the other side of water and don't know how to get back!

Examiner Comments

This is a good attempt at a story, but due to the erratic control shown is held in Band 2. There are numerous errors, particularly in the use (or absence) of past tenses, as well as problems with word order in sentences. Some effort is required by the reader.

Band: 2

SAMPLE H (Test 2, Question 8: 'An exciting adventure')

An exciting Adventure

Last january I travelled, with a friend, by car during 33 days in Brasil.

In this trip we visited a lot of places and we saw many beatiful things

At the begining we had to drive more than 4.000 km to get into the first beach. When we arrived we drank lots of beers to celebrate the first part of our trip.

We were very tired because we had been driving for 42 hours.

After that we went to other beach. We ate fish with vegetables and fruit juice right after we had drunk 20 beers!

To summarize our exciting trip, we spent one month travelling, drinking beer and visiting the beachs of the Brazilian coast.

Examiner Comments

This is a very good answer, showing confident and ambitious use of language. The story, a first-person narrative, is appropriate to the title and is well organised. There is a good range of accurately-produced tenses and some range of vocabulary. Errors are minor, non-impeding and mainly in spelling, for example, *begining...beachs.*

Band: 5

SAMPLE I (Test 2, Question 8: 'An exciting adventure')

An Excited Adventure

Long time ago. I was in Colombia with my best friend and her boyfriend, and we wanted to do something different becuase everithing was boring at our age, so we rented a car, started to drive around the country and finally we arrived to cartagena, with only £50 each, then we rented a small boat, went to an island in to the pacific ocean, we camping in the midle of the beach about 10 days. We fished, cooked, swam, oh! we really enjoyed that, and when we come back our parents wanted to kill us! They were very worried and upset with us, I'm felt very bad, and gave they an apologiaze, but now we laughing, remember our first trip.

Examiner Comments

This is an adequate attempt, although the mis-copying in the title is an unfortunate start. There are a number of mainly non-impeding errors and the range used is adequate for the task set. There is some attempt at organisation, including a suitable ending (even if inaccurately produced).

Band: 3

PAPER 2   LISTENING

Part 1

1 C   2 C   3 C   4 A   5 C   6 A   7 A

Part 2

8 C   9 B   10 B   11 A   12 C   13 A

Part 3

(*Recognisable spelling accepted in number 16*)
14 (of) March
15 talk(s)
16 computer program(s)/programme(s)
17 Saturday
18 (full)(-)(time) student(s)
19 984 7711

Part 4

20 B   21 A   22 B   23 A   24 A   25 B

Test 2 transcript

This is the Cambridge Preliminary English Test number 2. There are four parts to the test. You will hear each part twice.

For each part of the test, there will be time for you to look through the questions and time for you to check your answers.

Write your answers on the question paper. You will have six minutes at the end of the test to copy your answers on to the answer sheet.

The recording will now be stopped. Please ask any questions now because you must not speak during the test.

[pause]

PART 1   Now open your question paper and look at Part 1.

There are seven questions in this part. For each question there are three pictures and a short recording. Choose the correct picture and put a tick in the box below it.

Before we start, here is an example.

What's the time?

Woman: Have you got the time?
Man: Yes, it's twenty past three.

[pause]

The first picture is correct so there is a tick in box A.

Look at the three pictures for question 1 now.

[pause]

Now we are ready to start. Listen carefully. You will hear each recording twice.

One. When and where are they meeting?

Woman: What time are we meeting Jane?
Man: At half past seven outside the restaurant.
Woman: I told her to wait inside, at a table.
Man: I know, but she said she'd prefer to meet us outside.

[pause]

Now listen again.

[The recording is repeated.]

[pause]

Two. What will Chris get for his birthday?

Girl: It's Chris's birthday on Friday. What shall we get him?
Boy: Mmm, it's difficult. Tapes? CDs? But he's already got a lot of those …
Girl: We could get him something to wear. No, let's get him a book on sport –
        he's really keen on that.
Boy: Why not?

[pause]

Now listen again.

[The recording is repeated.]

[pause]

Three. What does Mr Jones look like?

Man: So, could you describe Mr Jones for me please, madam?
Woman: Well, he's about 40 years old, bald, with a moustache. He's got large
             ears and he wears glasses.

[pause]

Now listen again.

[The recording is repeated.]

[pause]

Four. Where is he going to plant the tree?

Woman: Where are you going to plant the tree? By the front door?
Man: No, that would be silly. It'll grow too big. I'm going to put it at the back
             of the garage. When it's grown, it'll give us some shade in the summer.
Woman: I thought it would be better right at the other end of the lawn.
Man: Oh, no.

[pause]

Now listen again.

[The recording is repeated.]

[pause]

Five. What is the man going to buy?

Man: Shall I get some fruit for the picnic?
Woman: Yes, can you get some oranges and bananas?
Man: I'm not very keen on oranges. How about grapes instead?
Woman: They're so expensive at the moment. Just get the bananas.

[pause]

Now listen again.

[The recording is repeated.]

[pause]

Six. Which is Gary's room?

Woman: Look, Gary's sent us a postcard of his hotel, and he's put a cross to
            show us his window!
Man: Ah, right in the middle.
Woman: Yes, he says he wanted a room on the top floor, but the only room
            available was on the floor below that.

[pause]

Now listen again.

[The recording is repeated.]

[pause]

Seven. Which is the best vehicle for the man?

Woman: Good morning, sir, how can I help you?
Man: Well, I'd like to hire a car, please. Something fast and comfortable, with
            enough room for four adults and a child.

[pause]

Now listen again.

[The recording is repeated.]

[pause]

That is the end of Part 1.

[pause]

PART 2   *Now turn to Part 2, questions 8–13.*

You will hear a recorded message about an arts festival.

*For each question, put a tick in the correct box. You now have 45 seconds to
look at the questions for Part 2.*

[pause]

Now we are ready to start. Listen carefully. You will hear the recording twice.

Message: This is the Arts Festival Box Office. There is no one here to take your
              call, but do not hang up, as further information follows.

The Festival begins on the 12th of May and continues to the 28th. There are things happening in several parts of the town itself, and outside it.

At the Theatre Royal, there will be a series of concerts, starting with jazz singer Elaine Delmar on the 12th of May. George Melly brings his own special kind of jazz and fun to the theatre on the 13th of May. On Thursday the 19th of May, there is the opera *Faust*. For classical music fans, the Brodsky String Quartet appear on the 23rd of May.

There are also concerts at the Corn Exchange. For people who prefer dance music, we have the London All Stars Steel Band on Sunday the 15th of May. On Thursday the 19th of May we welcome back the Viennese Gala Orchestra, who are regular performers at the Festival. Finally, also at the Corn Exchange, there will be a series of jazz concerts each Friday at 1 o'clock. During these lunch-time concerts a bar will be open for the sale of wine and we are offering free soft drinks. Sandwiches will also be on sale. Light meals can be bought in the restaurant afterwards.

There are various other musical performances in the cathedral, and poetry readings in one of the town's churches. The Film Society has arranged to show a film of Mozart's opera *Don Giovanni* at the theatre. Our programme has full details.

Ickworth House, just outside the town, is joining in the Festival as usual. There is a guided walk around Ickworth Park on Sunday the 15th, which will last about two and a half hours. Also, on the 19th of May, we have a special concert of piano music, given by Oliver Davies in the beautiful Ickworth Library. The price of tickets includes coffee and biscuits and you are advised to book early, as this is always especially popular.

For more information, send for our Festival programme or visit the Box Office from 10.00 a.m. to 8 p.m. Mondays to Fridays, or 12.00 to 8 p.m. on Saturdays. Bookings can be made in person (cash, cheque or credit card), by post (cheques only), or by telephone (credit cards only). We also accept credit card bookings by fax, on 0284 706035. For these bookings, you must use our booking form.

Thank you for calling.

[pause]

Now listen again.

That is the end of Part 2.

[pause]

PART 3   *Now turn to Part 3, questions 14–19.*

You will hear someone talking on the radio about a Language Study Fair.

For each question, fill in the missing information in the numbered space.

You now have 20 seconds to look at Part 3.

[pause]

Key

Now we are ready to start. Listen carefully. You will hear the recording twice.

Organiser: If you're studying English, the Language Study Fair that's being held this month will certainly interest you. The show is taking place between the 17th and 19th of March at the National Education Centre. It aims to answer all your questions about self-study (that's studying by yourself), whatever your level.

The Language Study Fair provides a perfect opportunity for you to see, compare and get advice on everything that's available to help you improve the way you study. Over 350 leading producers of educational materials will be present. Come along to this, and you won't waste your money in the future on materials that are out-of-date, or books that you just don't need.

We've got lots of different things for you to see and hear. There will be stands showing different types of self-study textbooks and talks by educational speakers on the best ways to study by yourself. You'll be able to see the latest furniture available for people who study at home. We're sure you'll also enjoy watching people using the latest computer programs, which can make studying English alone so much easier.

This is your chance to make good decisions about what you buy. You can attend the fair between nine-thirty and five on Thursday and Friday, and from nine-thirty to four on Saturday.

Tickets cost £5 each, or £3 if you're a full-time student. All tickets can be booked by ringing the ticket hotline. The number is 984 7711. Parking can be really difficult around the National Education Centre. However, an all-day space can be booked for only £2.50 per vehicle.

So, we look forward to seeing you there!

[pause]

Now listen again.

[The recording is repeated.]

That is the end of Part 3.

[pause]

PART 4 *Now turn to Part 4, questions 20–25.*

Look at the six sentences for this part. You will hear a conversation between a girl, Kate, and a boy, George.

Decide if each sentence is correct or incorrect. If it is correct, put a tick in the box under A for YES. If it is not correct, put a tick in the box under B for NO.

You now have 20 seconds to look at the questions for Part 4.

[pause]

Now we are ready to start. Listen carefully. You will hear the recording twice.

Kate: I don't remember much of that lecture. The doctor gave me this medicine for my cough, but I don't like it – it seems to make me awfully sleepy and I can't follow my lectures.

George: Well, if you don't take it, none of us will be able to follow our lectures – all we'll hear is you coughing!

Kate: Oh dear, do you think I'll annoy everybody?

George: Yes. You could study at home for a couple of days – you know, have some time off until it gets better.

Kate: Oh I couldn't do that! I'd miss too much and I get really uncomfortable when I have a lot of catching up to do. Last year I missed a whole week when I fell off my bike and had that enormous bandage on my hand. It took me ages to do all the work when I came back.

George: Oh, you worry too much. You can work at home. Just get Mr Gray to tell you which parts of the coursebook we'll be covering and read it yourself at home. All he does is go through the book anyway – you might as well do it yourself.

Kate: Oh, that's a bit unfair! I think Mr Gray's really nice. He's always willing to stay behind after class if you don't understand something.

George: Being 'really nice' and never in a hurry doesn't make him a good lecturer. Anyway I think you should look after your health first – and ours! If we sit in that small, hot room with you for the next three days, we'll all have your cough by the end of it.

Kate: Mmm, perhaps you're right. I don't care about myself, but I wouldn't like other people to blame me for their illnesses. I have got a bit of a temperature now, too – so maybe I'll go and see Mr Gray after lunch and tell him I won't be at this afternoon's lecture.

George: Or the *next* two … come on, you've got to get better.

Kate: I suppose you're right.

George: Then we can all go out as we planned at the weekend.

Kate: OK then, I don't want to miss that … and I *do* feel ill …

[pause]

Now listen again.

[The recording is repeated.]

That is the end of Part 4.

[pause]

You now have six minutes to check and copy your answers on to the answer sheet.

Note: Teacher, stop the tape here and time six minutes. Remind students when there is **one** minute remaining.

That is the end of the test.

Test 3

PAPER 1   READING AND WRITING

READING

Part 1

1 B   2 A   3 C   4 B   5 C

Part 2

6 H   7 A   8 F   9 C   10 E

Part 3

| 11 A | 12 A | 13 B | 14 B | 15 B | 16 B | 17 A |
| 18 B | 19 A | 20 A | | | | |

Part 4

21 B   22 D   23 C   24 C   25 A

Part 5

| 26 C | 27 D | 28 A | 29 B | 30 C | 31 B | 32 A |
| 33 D | 34 B | 35 A | | | | |

WRITING

Part 1

1 Nearly every seat was taken in the cinema.

| **There weren't** | many seats (left) | **in the cinema.** |

2 Jane had a worse seat than Dave.

| **Dave had** | a better seat | **than Jane.** |

3 Jane couldn't see the screen very well.

| **Jane found** | it difficult/hard | **to see the screen.** |

4 Dave said that he had seen the film before.

| **Dave said: 'I** | have/'ve | (already) seen | **this film before.'** |

5 They spent two hours watching the film.

| **The film** | lasted | **for two hours.** |

Part 2

Task-specific Mark scheme

The postcard should incorporate the following points:

i   why the student has moved

ii some information on the facilities the town has

iii something the student dislikes about the town

The following sample answers can be used as a guide when marking.

SAMPLE A (Test 3, Question 6: Postcard to a penfriend)

Hi Susan I have sended this postcard to you because, I would like you to see how the town look like I'm sorry I havn't call you before I leave, because I hasn't got enough time and I didn't explained to you why I has to moved. The recent I has to moved because, my parent they're cheanged their job to this town that why I have moved over here. And this Town has a bevtyful old bliding. So I hope you will come and visit me soon.

Examiner Comments

One content element has been omitted (what the candidate dislikes about the town), so the answer can receive a maximum mark of 3. The other two elements are adequately dealt with, although language errors cause some effort to be required by the reader.

Band: 3

SAMPLE B (Test 3, Question 6: Postcard to a penfriend)

> Hello Joana. How are you?
>
> I hope you are fine.
>
> I have moved recently to this town because we have more opportunities to have a better life. We can travel far every where by public transport so faster as you can't imagine, and taxis are cheap too. If you want see the town you can buy a ticket for one day by bus and you could visit many monuments.
>
> The problem are the pickpockets we have to be carefull.

Examiner Comments

All content elements are covered appropriately. Although the answer exceeds the word limit, the content is wholly relevant. Language errors are present, but don't impede the reading of the message.

Band: 5

SAMPLE C (Test 3, Question 6: Postcard to a penfriend)

Dear my friend,

I'm in a new town. I had an offer my old boss. It was a good opportunity for me. So I decided to move that country. It is a good place but I don't like living here. I have already missed my country. I think people who lives here isn't friendly and I don't like the weather. During the day some times it's sunny and sometimes it's rainy.

Can you come here in December in your free time. We can have a good time especially at the weekends. There were lots of historical places here and we can go some interesting places in the nights. We saw lots of places.

Examiner Comments

All three content elements are adequately dealt with, but the length of the answer and the language errors affect the clarity of the message slightly, requiring occasional effort by the reader.

Band: 4

Part 3

The following sample answers can be used as a guide when marking.

SAMPLE D (Test 3, Question 7: 'It was a fantastic party')

> It was a fantastic party. I hadn't expected it will be so cool! There were a lot of people from our school I hadn't met before. We danced, spoke, drunk a bit and there was very friendly atmosphere. I meet there my old friends I hadn't see since my birthday. All of us enjoed the party till the moment when parents of the hoste of the party sudenly came back from their trip they had started crying and soon, one by one, we all slipped out of the house, and afterwards, having considered the situation decided don't pay much intention to the incident and to go to continue our evening at enouthere place

Examiner Comments

This is a good attempt, showing confident and ambitious use of language, which, with fewer errors, would have achieved Band 5. Errors are non-impending, though cause a little effort to be rerquired by the reader. There is a good range of structures and vocabulary and some natural expression, for example, *... one by one, we all slipped out of the house ...*

Band: 4

Key

SAMPLE E (Test 3, Question 7: 'It was a fantastic party')

It was a fantastic party. I'm arrived at 9 o'clock and met a so many people from differents countries, I spoke with a Italian girl about her country and she told me some difference with a London, I told her about Colombian and the differents places that she can know and the differents cultures in the same country.

I danced with a lot of girls but one of them impact me, she was dressing with a sexy clothes and she looked beatifull she's from Sweden her name is Solveie she was studing enginering. She gave me her phone number but I lose it.

I went to home at 3 am, I'm tired and slept till 11 am.

Examiner Comments

This is an adequate attempt at a story, though contains a number of non-impeding errors, particularly in tense formation, agreement and spelling. There is some attempt at organisation, although sentence structure is unwieldy at times.

Band: 3

SAMPLE F (Test 3, Question 7: 'It was a fantastic party')

It was a fantastic party. To now I can remember when I was eighteen years old, I take part in a big part. It was for new student of university and hold by university authority. I was very happy at that party because I had made a lot of friend in that party. Then some of them become my classmate. We were dancing beer song, and drank. Oh It's a very fantastic party. We are talking about our future. I didn't what time a girl had joined us. She said that she would like become a famous modal and designer. She's very beatiful and she told she's very happy that night. Then we became a good friend, espically me. I always invite hime to climb mountain visity place ... . Before long time we in love each other. I very love him, and he is too. We have planed our future together. I think I'll got married soon. When I thought about that party I alway say that was a fantastic party.

Examiner Comments

The story requires some effort by the reader, mainly due to the high number of errors. The language is quite ambitious and there is some evidence of range, though this is marred by errors, for example *It was for new student of university and hold by university authority.*

Band: 2

SAMPLE G (Test 3, Question 8: Letter to a friend)

> I'm looking for a great concerts but at the moment I can't find. Are here any interesting place for visit? Sometimes I was very bored like you, but at the moment I can say that I know where are the interesting places for visit and sometimes I go a great concert that pop music, for example this weeked I'll going to a special place where all time everybody are enjoy and are soo friendly. So, if you want to come here. come, just come that's it.
>
> Bye.

Examiner Comments

This is a poor attempt, containing little information of relevance to the reader. It is difficult to understand at times, due to the lack of basic control.

Band: 1

SAMPLE H **(Test 3, Question 8: Letter to a friend)**

Hello!!!

Do you know about music? Well, I will answer, firts, in my country, there are a types of music very different, depends If you stay in a cold city or a sunny city you will meet differents styles, but I prefer the latin music, because I love to dance!!! In my country, frewently do many concerts, but, depends the styles, can be romantic, pop music, latin music, salsa ... electronic music, you can find and get your preferents. In my personal opinion, I prefer to listen to pop music, I like madonna, aerosmith, bon jovi and I like too spanish music, you know! I speak spanish ...

And, I have a colection about the famous songs, I can give you, and you can listen to ... and then, you'll say me, what as you prefer? or what kind of music would you like? and why not, If you like latin music, If you want to learn to dance, I can teach you!!! It's very easy, you only need to try!!! Well, I'll send you my colection and I hope your answer as soon as possible.

Kisses!!!

Examiner Comments

This is an informative letter, showing fairly ambitious use of language. The letter is well organised, with some linking of sentences. There is a more than adequate range of structures and vocabulary, as well as some appropriately chatty expressions. There are, however, some non-impending errrors.

Band: 4

SAMPLE I **(Test 3, Question 8: Letter to a friend)**

> Dear Olga,
>
> I am very happy to receive your letter I would like to write you some information about music in Poland.
>
> At summer there are a lot of concerts in the biggest cities of Poland, and people all days sitting at parks and listening to a lot of kind of music. It is very interesting way to spend free time for everybody who like music. In my country there is not special kind of music — it is similar to another countries, but it is very good idea, because you can choose this music concerts what you like.
>
> At Warsaw this mounth it will be held some pop music concerts and if you like instrumental music — you can listen to it, too.
>
> I like instrumental music, and that is why — I write you about it.
>
> In the end this mount it will be very interesting concert instrumental music in Royal Park in Warsaw.
>
> I would like to invite you — if you want.
>
> I am waiting for you answer.
>
> Buy Reneta

Examiner Comments

This is a good attempt at the task, with ambitious use of language and some range of relevant vocabulary. However, it is flawed by a number of errors, which are mainly non-impeding, for example *At Warsaw this mounth it will be held ...* The answer requires some effort by the reader.

Band: 3

PAPER 2   LISTENING

Part 1

1 B   2 C   3 A   4 B   5 C   6 A   7 C

Part 2

8 C   9 A   10 C   11 C   12 B   13 C

Part 3

(*Recognisable spelling accepted in numbers 16, 17 and 19*)
14 (a) family
15 six/6 months
16 (a) receptionist
17 (a) bakery/baker's
18 four/(0)4/4 o'clock/am/a.m./in the morning
19 foreign/Foreign/Department/department/Desk/desk

Part 4

20 B   21 B   22 A   23 A   24 A   25 B

Test 3 transcript

This is the Cambridge Preliminary English Test number 3. There are four parts to the test. You will hear each part twice.

For each part of the test, there will be time for you to look through the questions and time for you to check your answers.

Write your answers on the question paper. You will have six minutes at the end of the test to copy your answers on to the answer sheet.

The recording will now be stopped. Please ask any questions now because you must not speak during the test.

[pause]

PART 1   *Now open your question paper and look at Part 1.*

There are seven questions in this part. For each question there are three pictures and a short recording. Choose the correct picture and put a tick in the box below it.

Before we start, here is an example.

What's the time?

Woman: Have you got the time?
Man: Yes, it's twenty past three.

[pause]

The first picture is correct so there is a tick in box A.

Key

Look at the three pictures for question 1 now.

[pause]

Now we are ready to start. Listen carefully. You will hear each recording twice.

One. Where is the station?

Woman: Excuse me, can you tell us the way to the station?
Man: Take the second on the right and it's at the end of that road.

[pause]

Now listen again.

[The recording is repeated.]

[pause]

Two. Where did the woman put the calculator?

Man: Have you used my calculator?
Woman: Yes, can't you find it? I put it back on the desk.
Man: Where?
Woman: Next to the lamp, I think. No, wait a minute, it's on that pile of books.

[pause]

Now listen again.

[The recording is repeated.]

[pause]

Three. Where is Helen?

Man: Is Helen here?
Woman: Yes, she's over there, next to the man in the shorts.
Man: Who's that with her?
Woman: Her brother, I think.

[pause]

Now listen again.

[The recording is repeated.]

[pause]

Four. Which building was hit by lightning?

Man 1: Did you hear the storm last night?
Man 2: Of course. It was right over our apartment and seemed to hit something near the hotel.
Man 1: Yes, the factory near the church was hit by lightning. It's lucky no one was at work.

[pause]

Now listen again.

[The recording is repeated.]

[pause]

130

Five. What does the woman want to buy?

Woman: Now I've bought this skirt, I think I need some new shoes to go with it.

Man: Can't you wear your boots?

Woman: No, they're too old. I think it would look better with flat shoes.

Man: Come on then, let's try that shop over the road.

[pause]

Now listen again.

[The recording is repeated.]

[pause]

Six. Which picture does the woman decide to send?

Woman: My mother wants me to send her a photo of our new house. Which one shall I send?

Man: This one is nice, with the children playing in the back garden.

Woman: I prefer this one with you standing by the front door.

Man: Well, send her that one then.

[pause]

Now listen again.

[The recording is repeated.]

[pause]

Seven. Which hotel has the man chosen?

Woman: Have you decided which hotel you're going to stay in?

Man: Oh yes. It's the largest in the area, it's got four floors and it's right on the seashore ... *and* there's an outdoor pool as well. So we'll be able to swim every day.

[pause]

Now listen again.

[The recording is repeated.]

[pause]

That is the end of Part 1.

[pause]

Key

PART 2   *Now turn to Part 2, questions 8–13.*
You will hear a radio interview with a man who works on an international camp.

For each question, put a tick in the correct box. You now have 45 seconds to look at the questions for Part 2.

[pause]

Now we are ready to start. Listen carefully. You will hear the recording twice.

Presenter: Hi there. On last week's programme we interviewed the man behind the idea of the International Camps. So I thought that this week you'd be interested to hear more about one of the Camps which will be held later this year. Over to you, Michael …

Michael: Thank you. Yes, the Camp is open to everyone between the ages of 18 to 23. You don't have to be a student – you don't even have to be employed, but you must be able to speak one foreign language in addition to your mother tongue.

Presenter: OK. And what about accommodation?

Michael: Well, the International Camp organisers supply tents which sleep up to four people but you are unlikely to know the people who you'll be sharing a tent with. The nationalities are mixed, so you'll be sharing with people who may not even speak your language!

Presenter: Sounds interesting. Who does the cooking at the Camp?

Michael: Everybody is expected to help with the running of the Camp. That means helping to prepare food, keeping the camp site clean and tidy, and so on. The Camp organisers are looking for people who can get along with others whatever happens.

Presenter: And is there anything you need to take?

Michael: Well as I've said, tents are provided but you'll need to bring your own pillow, knife, fork and spoon. If you get chosen, you're also asked to bring along photographs, postcards – anything that shows some of the traditions and customs of your own country. Everything goes into an exhibition at the start of the Camp, together with a huge map of the world showing the different countries people come from.

Presenter: And is there any entertainment?

Michael: Yes, there is. Everyone helps to provide the Camp entertainment. You are expected to sing, dance or play something musical – it doesn't matter how good or bad you are. There is a space on the form to write down what you can do.

Presenter: Sounds great fun. And what does it all cost?

Michael: Well, you have to find your own way to the Camp, so it's up to you whether you fly, cycle, walk, hitch-hike or whatever. The charge for a week's Camp is 300 dollars, but you'll have to change that into your own currency to get a better idea of the cost. You have to pay the full cost before you arrive, but you can pay in any currency you want or you can use a credit card if you have one. Right. Now for the phone number to ring …

[pause]

Now listen again.

[The recording is repeated.]

That is the end of Part 2.

[pause]

PART 3 *Now turn to Part 3, questions 14–19.*

You will hear a young woman who has applied for an office job talking about her jobs abroad.

For each question, fill in the missing information in the numbered space.

You now have 20 seconds to look at Part 3.

[pause]

Now we are ready to start. Listen carefully. You will hear the recording twice.

Interviewer: Hello, Miss Brownlow, come and sit down. Now, I'd like you to tell me more about the two years you spent abroad after leaving school.

Woman: Oh, right. Well, I decided to go abroad to see the world. I only intended staying for six months but in the end I stayed two years. First of all I worked for a family. I looked after their three children – all under the age of ten so I was kept very busy! I really liked the family, but after six months I was ready for a change although I didn't want to come home. Then I applied for a job in a hotel as a receptionist. That way I could still practise my languages. And it was really good because I had my own room in the hotel and I had all my meals there as well. And then the hotel closed down! But the manager offered me a job – in a bakery – it belonged to his brother – and I worked there for almost a year. At the beginning it was really hard because I had to get up so early in the morning – around four o'clock every day. But once I got used to that, it was great, because I'd finished work by two o'clock in the afternoon and the rest of the time was my own. But my parents thought I ought to come home and get a 'proper job'. I suppose they were right. So that's when I applied for the job with the Bank International in their foreign department and so I continued to use my languages.

Interviewer: You've had quite a lot of experience, haven't you! Now, if I could ask you …

[pause]

Now listen again.

[The recording is repeated.]

That is the end of Part 3.

[pause]

133

Key

PART 4 Now turn to Part 4, questions 20–25.

Look at the six sentences for this part. You will hear a conversation between a father and his daughter, Sonia.

Decide if each sentence is correct or incorrect. If it is correct, put a tick in the box under A for YES. If it is not correct, put a tick in the box under B for NO.

You now have 20 seconds to look at the questions for Part 4.

[pause]

Now we are ready to start. Listen carefully. You will hear the recording twice.

Father: So – this time next week you'll be eighteen!
Sonia: I can't believe it.
Father: Neither can I – you don't seem a day over ten!
Sonia: Thank you!
Father: Anyway, have you thought what you'd like for your birthday?
Sonia: Well, I wondered whether I could have driving lessons.
Father: But we don't have a car!
Sonia: I know, but it would be useful to know how for when I have my own car.
Father: But you're still at school. How could you afford a car?!
Sonia: But most people in my class are having driving lessons.
Father: Well maybe their parents can afford a car. There's no point in having lessons if you can't practise.
Sonia: Maria says I can practise with her family's car.
Father: Oh, so you've discussed it with Maria! And I wonder what her parents would say if they knew. Do you know how much car insurance costs?
Sonia: Yes – it's expensive. But I could get a job on Saturday or Sunday and help pay for it. If I could drive I could probably get a job more easily – you know, delivering things or taking people to places.
Father: Yes – why not – my daughter Sonia with her own taxi service! Where do you think you're going to get a car?
Sonia: I thought I would drive other people's.
Father: Look, I know you want to be like your friends but it's not sensible to think of driving until you can afford your own car. Why don't I pay for you to have a lesson so that you can see what it's like? And, if the day ever comes when I'm rich, I'll be happy to help you buy a car. Now – what would you like for your birthday?
Sonia: OK, Dad – you win! But I'd still like to begin saving. Anyway, until then what I'd really like would be to go out to dinner with you and Mum to save Mum cooking.
Father: That's a good idea and I'll tell you what – we'll go by taxi!

[pause]

Now listen again.

[The recording is repeated.]

That is the end of Part 4.

[pause]

You now have six minutes to check and copy your answers on to the answer sheet.

Note: Teacher, stop the tape here and time six minutes. Remind students when there is **one** minute remaining.

That is the end of the test.

134

Test 4

PAPER 1   READING AND WRITING

READING

Part 1

1 B   2 B   3 C   4 C   5 A

Part 2

6 C   7 F   8 D   9 H   10 A

Part 3

11 B   12 A   13 B   14 B   15 B   16 A   17 A
18 B   19 A   20 A

Part 4

21 A   22 A   23 C   24 D   25 B

Part 5

26 D   27 B   28 C   29 A   30 A   31 D   32 A
33 D   34 C   35 A

WRITING

Part 1

1 My appointment with Dr Gibson is at ten o'clock.

At ten o'clock I am	going to have	**an appointment with Dr Gibson.**

2 This office is Dr Gibson's.

This office	belongs	**to Dr Gibson.**

3 Dr Gibson told me to take off my shoes and socks.

Dr Gibson said: 'Please take	your shoes	**and socks off.'**

4 'It would be a good idea to take more exercise.'

'You really	ought/need	**to take more exercise.'**

5 I was given some information about a local gym.

The hospital	gave me	**some information about a local gym.**

Part 2

Task-specific Mark scheme

The e-mail should incorporate the following points:

i   explanation of the good news
ii feelings about the news
iii enquiry about friend's family.

The following sample answers can be used as a guide when marking.

SAMPLE A (Test 4, Question 6: e-mail to a friend)

How are you?
I'm very well.
How are (the) your family?
I've got some good news about my exam.
In the middle of July, I took exam that to enter the university.
Yesterday I received good result about that.
So. I'm going to go to the university at next term of course really nice.

Examiner Comments

This is a good answer, dealing with all three content elements almost within the word limit. However, the line-by-line presentation of the sentences affects the readability of the message slightly. The message also ends rather suddenly.

Band: 4

SAMPLE B **(Test 4, Question 6: e-mail to a friend)**

Hi,

I have got a good news. Next week I am going to go your country. I saved my money to work part time job. and already booked the ticket So I am so extied that. we can meet soon.

Examiner Comments

In this script, the first two content elements are sucessfully dealt with, but the third (asking about the reader's family) has been omitted. The script can only receive 3, therefore. Language errors are minor and do not affect the clarity of the message, such as it is.

Band: 3

SAMPLE C (Test 4, Question 6: e-mail to a friend)

Hi! How are you? Yesterday, I passed a examination, so I can go the upper class. I'd been afraid that I didn't pass it, but I could. I can't believe it. How about you? Is anything special?

By the way, how are your parents? It is long time since I met them. Please say hello to them.

I'll write soon, bye bye.

Takako

Examiner Comments

This is an excellent attempt, covering all three content elements appropriately. Although the writer has slightly exceeded the word limit, the content is relevant and natural. The answer reads well and requires no effort by the reader.

Band: 5

Part 3

The following sample answers can be used as a guide when marking.

SAMPLE D (Test 4, Question 7: Letter to a penfriend)

> Hi!
>
> Thank you for your letter. Learning English is still interesting and it is very good for me. I have good English teacher and also good classmates. They make me more interest to learn English.
>
> Let me introduce my English class.
>
> There are eleven nice students and one nice teacher.
>
> The nice teacher's name is Pete! He is tall, handsome. Furthermore, he makes us very interest and feel comfortable in his class.
>
> It is time to talk about my classmates!
>
> They are all women except one man and they have variety nationality. For example South Korea (of course include me), Japan, Poland, Columbia and China etc.
>
> Most of them have cheerful character and passion to learn English.
>
> That is why I said that I like learning English.
>
> I will send a letter soon again.
>
> Take it easy!!

Examiner Comments

This is a good attempt, showing fairly ambitious use of language and with evidence of some range, for example *cheerful character … passion to learn English*. Sentence structure is sound and there is some linking of sentences. The answer requires only a little effort by the reader.

Band: 4

SAMPLE E **(Test 4, Question 7: Letter to a penfriend)**

Dear Edwin,

I'm glad receive news your,
I'm studying in Stanton School, my class starts
about twelve o'clock, and it finishes at three
o'clock. I have two teachers, the first one for first
two hours, and he teaches about grammar and the
second one is speaking teacher both are good
teacher and very kind.

There are about fifteen students, fourteen gils and
me, they are cheerfuly, we usually go to pub the
fridays. The english classes are good I've learned
a lot english, the classes are interesting and you
can discuss about you country and culture, and
you can know differents habits.
I hope that you will happy with my answer,
*   Bye.*
*   Manuel*

Examiner Comments

This is an adequate answer with some attempt at organisation, although the linking of sentences isn't always maintained and sentence structure isn't totally sound. There are a number of non-impeding errors within an adequate range of structures and vocabulary.

Band: 3

SAMPLE F (Test 4, Question 7: Letter to a penfriend)

Hallo Dear Ann!
I'm going to school everyday from 12 – 3 pm. I've got
two teachers first one for two hours – he's teaching
us gramma, reading, and the second he's teaching us
speaking, vocabulary. Everyday is very interesting and
I'm finding out something new about langvage and
culture. There isn't in the classe people from my
country so I can speek English all the time. After
classes we've got social program, so we're also meeting
at the evenings and speeking English.

Examiner Comments

This answer is slightly short at 77 words. The language used is a little simple at times and there are a number of non-impeding errors, particularly in tenses and spelling. There is some attempt at organising the letter, although there is no closing formula or suitable final sentence.

Band: 2

SAMPLE G (Test 4, Question 8: 'A broken window')

> "A broken window"
>
> Something strange had happened me yesterday. It was after my work, me and my friend we were sitting and watching TV, it was very quiet outside. Sudenly something broke my window and I found it on my carpet. I came clouser and It was stone. I clouse to my window and I didn't sow nobodhy outside. We have decided to call the police, but after we went out the house and sow four men who were building a house next to mine. They explained that it was an accident on the building and they so sorry and promise to fix up the window tomorrow, but I said what about tonight? My friend offer my one night at her place.

Examiner Comments

This is quite a good attempt at writing a story, showing some range and ambition, but it is flawed by a number of non-impeding errors in tenses, use of articles, and spelling. It requires some effort by the reader.

Band: 3

SAMPLE H **(Test 4, Question 8: 'A broken window')**

> A broken window
>
> I take a English class everyday. My school in the oxford street that Central London and my teacher just live near here.
>
> one day when I arrived classroom, I found something strange condition because the room looks too dack even I turn on the light. Suddnly I heard my teacher's voice from out side. Just in that time I know the caturn changed to dack blue colours. when.

Examiner Comments

At only 69 words, this answer is too short and is clearly unfinished. The story does not actually refer to a broken window, although does appear to have some relevance to the title. However, because of impeding errors, it is difficult to understand.

Band: 1

SAMPLE I (Test 4, Question 8: 'A broken window')

> This is a story of my english teacher's holiday. On last Sunday, he stayed at home with his son. and wife. After lunch, he went to the park in front of the house with his son, and was playing baseball. His son Tomy wants to be a baseball player in the future. So, he always played the baseball with his friends. But, on this day, Tomy was playing with his father. Mike wasn't good at the baseball. Tomy threw a ball, and Mike hit it!! The ball that Mike had hit broke a window of his house. of course, his wife lost her temper. He apologized for her. His wife said "It's ok. I don't mind. But, you must tidy up here. and from today, make meals on your own!!"
> She was really angry.

Examiner Comments

This is a good story, showing fairly ambitious use of language and some range of structures and vocabulary, as well as some suitable expressions, for example *lost her temper ... tidy up*. The story is well organised and there is some linking of sentences.

Band: 4

PAPER 2   LISTENING

Part 1

1 A   2 C   3 A   4 C   5 A   6 C   7 C

Part 2

8 C   9 A   10 B   11 B   12 C   13 B

Part 3

(*Recognisable spelling accepted in numbers 15 and 17*)
14 (the) north(-)west/North(-)West
15 poet
16 (short) stories
17 waitress
18 (')City Life(')
19 24/twenty(-)four

Part 4

20 B   21 A   22 B   23 A   24 A   25 A

Test 4 transcript

This is the Cambridge Preliminary English Test number 4. There are four parts to the test. You will hear each part twice.

For each part of the test, there will be time for you to look through the questions and time for you to check your answers.

Write your answers on the question paper. You will have six minutes at the end of the test to copy your answers on to the answer sheet.

The recording will now be stopped. Please ask any questions now because you must not speak during the test.

[pause]

PART 1   *Now open your question paper and look at Part 1.*

There are seven questions in this part. For each question there are three pictures and a short recording. Choose the correct picture and put a tick in the box below it.

Before we start, here is an example.

What's the time?

Woman: Have you got the time?
Man: Yes, it's twenty past three.

[pause]

The first picture is correct so there is a tick in box A.

Look at the three pictures for question 1 now.

[pause]

Now we are ready to start. Listen carefully. You will hear each recording twice.

One. Where are the woman's glasses?

Woman: I can never find my glasses!

Man: Where did you have them last?

Woman: I either had them when I was working, or I left them in the lounge when I was watching television.

Man: They're not in either of those places, you know – you're wearing them!

[pause]

Now listen again.

[The recording is repeated.]

[pause]

Two. What damage was done to the car?

Woman: I'm really annoyed. Someone's damaged my car again.

Man: Don't tell me someone's scratched the paint again!

Woman: No, not scratches this time. Someone's put paint all over the side.

[pause]

Now listen again.

[The recording is repeated.]

[pause]

Three. What did she bring?

Man: Did you remember to bring some toothpaste?

Woman: I think so. Wait a minute, I'll look … soap, towel, toothbrush. Er … no, sorry, I forgot.

[pause]

Now listen again.

[The recording is repeated.]

[pause]

Four. What did Sally buy?

Woman: I see you've been shopping, Sally. What have you got in the bag?

Sally: Well, I went into town to buy a new skirt, but I've come back with a T-shirt and a pair of jeans.

Woman: I thought you wanted some new shoes too.

Sally: Yes, I did. But I couldn't find any I liked.

[pause]

Now listen again.

[The recording is repeated.]

[pause]

Five. Where are the man and his grandma?

Man: Hello, Grandma, can I carry your case?
Grandma: Oh, that's nice of you. Thank you for coming to meet me. Travelling always makes me so nervous!
Man: Don't worry, we'll be in the car soon, and it won't take long to get home.
Grandma: Good, I'll be glad to get away from this noisy station.

[pause]

Now listen again.

[The recording is repeated.]

[pause]

Six. What would John like to be?

Teacher: What do you want to be when you leave school, John? You always wanted to be a professional footballer, didn't you?
Boy: Well, I did. I thought about being a doctor, too, but I don't think I could pass all the exams.
Teacher: What about being an engineer like your brother?
Boy: It's a nice idea – but I think I'd like to do what my dad does. He teaches maths.

[pause]

Now listen again.

[The recording is repeated.]

[pause]

Seven. Which pianist are the two people talking about?

Woman: I thought the most interesting pianist in the whole competition was Gavin Willow.
Man: Was he the tall one with long hair?
Woman: Well he was *tall*, but he had short, dark hair and a beard.
Man: Ah, yes, *I* know.

[pause]

Now listen again.

[The recording is repeated.]

[pause]

That is the end of Part 1.

[pause]

PART 2   *Now turn to Part 2, questions 8–13.*
You will hear a talk given to visitors to a fashion museum.

For each question, put a tick in the correct box. You now have 45 seconds to look at the questions for Part 2.

[pause]

Now we are ready to start. Listen carefully. You will hear the recording twice.

Guide: Welcome, ladies and gentlemen, to the Morecambe Museum of Fashion. Before we go up to the fashion exhibition 'Clothes of the Future', I would like to show you some slides on the screen, and say a few words about the history of fashion. I will also mention some of the important people in fashion. This will provide an introduction for you and will prepare you for the clothes that we're going to see in the exhibition.

As I'm sure you know, nowadays fashion is something that almost everybody enjoys. People of all age groups and all incomes usually have an interest in what they wear. But this has only recently happened, and I will tell you why.

Until the beginning of this century, it was only the rich who could afford to follow fashion. There were no factories to make many copies of the same article, as there are today. Rich men and women wore trousers, jackets and dresses which were made especially for them. This picture here shows a young lady being measured for a dress that she will have made by hand, exactly how she wants it to be. Ladies' clothes in those days were long and usually tight-fitting and made of heavy material.

However, the new century – the 1900s – brought new ideas. The important person at this time was Coco Chanel, who started making clothes in 1908, in Paris. Many people think she was the 20th century's most important influence on fashion. Chanel loved to wear loose-fitting clothes and produced jackets and skirts which everyone admired. Here's a picture of one of her ladies' suits. Even today people still wear styles like this when they want to look smart. Young Paris designers all began to produce simple clothes, and skirts started to get shorter.

The idea of special clothes for playing sports also became popular in the early 1920s. Things like long shorts and tennis clothes started to become fashionable. Soon factories produced these new styles more cheaply, and then many more people were able to enjoy fashion.

In 1947, after the second world war, Christian Dior used all the new materials available to produce a fashion which was known as the 'New Look'. As you can see in this picture, he made skirt lengths longer again.

Later, in the 60s, 'flower power' and student fashion were popular. In London, Mary Quant introduced short skirts. These were worn with boots that went up to the knee. Look at the white, shiny boots in this picture!

And now we come to today's exhibition. Some of the clothes you will see today will be very different from anything which you have seen before. The exhibition aims to take a look at the sort of clothes that we might wear in the next 50 years.

Let's go inside and have a look at the exciting clothes that are waiting for us …

[pause]

Now listen again.

[The recording is repeated.]

That is the end of Part 2.

[pause]

PART 3   *Now turn to Part 3, questions 14–19.*

You will hear a man talking about Tanya Perry's life.

For each question, fill in the missing information in the numbered space.

You now have 20 seconds to look at Part 3.

[pause]

Now we are ready to start. Listen carefully. You will hear the recording twice.

Interviewer: Hello and welcome. We're spending the first part of today's programme talking about Tanya Perry, and with me today is Ray Potter, her friend and colleague for many years …

Ray: Yes, well, I've known Tanya for nearly 20 years. Not many people know that she was born in London, in 1948. In 1952, her parents moved with Tanya and her brother to the north west. They lived in various places, before finally coming to Manchester in 1956.

Tanya spent a very happy period at school. In fact she was in the same class as Jack Peters, the famous poet. David Thompson, the artist, was also at the school – a couple of years below her, I think. So it was an interesting time for Tanya, who actually began to write short stories while she was at school. One of her stories appeared in the school magazine – I have a copy here. It's extraordinary, you can see a lot of her ideas starting to grow. When Tanya left school, she didn't go to university, as Jack Peters did, but got a job immediately. She was never interested in university life. What she wanted was to be part of the real world, to meet different people and get more experience of life. So in the early 1970s she became a waitress, working in what was then one of the most popular cafés in Manchester. She was writing at night and in 1975 she had her first play performed, at the Edinburgh Festival.

She gave up her day job the following year, to be able to write full-time. Several of her plays were performed, including one at the Court Theatre in London. This was where she met film director Robin Newgate, who she later married. Robin introduced her to the film world and, in 1979, she wrote the story which later became the film 'City Life', which Robin directed. It won the prize for best foreign film at an important French Film Festival in 1984.

Tanya could have moved to Hollywood then, but she was still married to the theatre – and to Robin – so she decided to stay here. Now she has 24 plays in print, 18 in translation, which makes her work very widely known all over the world.

[pause]

Now listen again.

[The recording is repeated.]

That is the end of Part 3.

[pause]

PART 4   *Now turn to Part 4, questions 20–25.*

Look at the six sentences for this part. You will hear a conversation between a man and a woman at home.

Decide if each sentence is correct or incorrect. If it is correct, put a tick in the box under A for YES. If it is not correct, put a tick in the box under B for NO.

You now have 20 seconds to look at the questions for Part 4.

[pause]

Now we are ready to start. Listen carefully. You will hear the recording twice.

Man: What shall we do tonight? Shall we go out somewhere?

Woman: No, I'm tired. I've had a really hard day.

Man: That's a bit boring! Come on, let's go to a cinema or see that new play at the theatre.

Woman: Not tonight. Why don't we rent a video and stay in?

Man: Well, I'd rather go out … but if you're tired … OK. So what shall we have? How about that new Italian film?

Woman: No, far too serious for me. I'd fall asleep! Why can't we get something funny – a film with Rik Moranis or someone like that.

Man: A comedy? No thanks. I'm not wasting my money.

Woman: Well, I'll pay, if you're going to be difficult about it.

Man: I'm not being difficult – I just don't want to see a comedy.

Woman: Fine. What else do you suggest then?

Man: How about a Robert de Niro?

Woman: We've seen them all.

Man: Maybe, but they're great films. Let's watch one again.

Woman: Now you're suggesting something that's a *real* waste of money! And I hate seeing films twice, you know that.

Man: OK, OK. What, then?

Woman: Oh, forget it. We're obviously not going to agree anyway!

Man: No, I tell you what, *you* go down to the video shop and choose a film. Whatever it is, I'll watch it.

Woman: Really? And you won't be difficult or make me feel guilty?

Man: No – go on, off you go. I'll make something to eat while you're out.

Woman: Great. See you in a few minutes then.

Man: Bye.

[pause]

Now listen again.

[The recording is repeated.]

That is the end of Part 4.

[pause]

You now have six minutes to check and copy your answers on to the answer sheet.

Note: Teacher, stop the tape here and time six minutes. Remind students when there is **one** minute remaining.

That is the end of the test.

Sample answer sheets

UNIVERSITY of CAMBRIDGE
ESOL Examinations

S A M P L E

Candidate Name
If not already printed, write name
in CAPITALS and complete the
Candidate No. grid (in pencil).

Candidate Signature

Examination Title

Centre

Supervisor:
If the candidate is ABSENT or has WITHDRAWN shade here

Centre No.

Candidate No.

Examination Details

0	0	0	0
1	1	1	1
2	2	2	2
3	3	3	3
4	4	4	4
5	5	5	5
6	6	6	6
7	7	7	7
8	8	8	8
9	9	9	9

PET Paper 1 Reading and Writing Candidate Answer Sheet 1

Instructions

Use a PENCIL (B or HB).

Rub out any answer you want to change with an eraser.

For **Reading:**
Mark ONE letter for each question.
For example, if you think **A** is the right answer to the
question, mark your answer sheet like this:

Part 1	**Part 2**	**Part 3**	**Part 4**	**Part 5**
1 A B C	6 A B C D E F G H	11 A B	21 A B C D	26 A B C D
2 A B C	7 A B C D E F G H	12 A B	22 A B C D	27 A B C D
3 A B C	8 A B C D E F G H	13 A B	23 A B C D	28 A B C D
4 A B C	9 A B C D E F G H	14 A B	24 A B C D	29 A B C D
5 A B C	10 A B C D E F G H	15 A B	25 A B C D	30 A B C D
		16 A B		31 A B C D
		17 A B		32 A B C D
		18 A B		33 A B C D
		19 A B		34 A B C D
		20 A B		35 A B C D

Continue on the other side of this sheet →

© UCLES/K&J   Photocopiable

For **Writing (Parts 1 and 2):**

Write your answers clearly in the spaces provided.

Part 1: Write your answers below.	Do not write here
1	1 1 0
2	1 2 0
3	1 3 0
4	1 4 0
5	1 5 0

Part 2 (Question 6): Write your answer below.

Put your answer to Writing Part 3 on Answer Sheet 2 ➡

UNIVERSITY *of* **CAMBRIDGE**
ESOL Examinations

Candidate Name
If not already printed, write name
in CAPITALS and complete the
Candidate No. grid (in pencil).

Candidate Signature

Examination Title

Centre

Supervisor:

If the candidate is ABSENT or has WITHDRAWN shade here ▭

Centre No.

Candidate No.

Examination Details

0	0	0	0
1	1	1	1
2	2	2	2
3	3	3	3
4	4	4	4
5	5	5	5
6	6	6	6
7	7	7	7
8	8	8	8
9	9	9	9

PET Paper 1 Reading and Writing   Candidate Answer Sheet 2

Candidate Instructions:

Write your answer to Writing Part 3
on the other side of this sheet.

→

Use a PENCIL (B or HB).

This section for use by FIRST Examiner only

Mark:

| 0 | 1.1 | 1.2 | 1.3 | 2.1 | 2.2 | 2.3 | 3.1 | 3.2 | 3.3 | 4.1 | 4.2 | 4.3 | 5.1 | 5.2 | 5.3 |

Examiner Number:

0	1	2	3	4	5	6	7	8	9
0	1	2	3	4	5	6	7	8	9
0	1	2	3	4	5	6	7	8	9
0	1	2	3	4	5	6	7	8	9

Part 3: Mark the number of the question you are answering here ➡ Q7 or Q8

Write your answer below.

Do not write below this line

This section for use by SECOND Examiner only

Mark:

0	1.1	1.2	1.3	2.1	2.2	2.3	3.1	3.2	3.3	4.1	4.2	4.3	5.1	5.2	5.3

Examiner Number:

	0 1 2 3 4 5 6 7 8 9
	0 1 2 3 4 5 6 7 8 9
	0 1 2 3 4 5 6 7 8 9
	0 1 2 3 4 5 6 7 8 9

UNIVERSITY *of* **CAMBRIDGE**
ESOL Examinations

SAMPLE

Candidate Name
If not already printed, write name
in CAPITALS and complete the
Candidate No. grid (in pencil).

Candidate Signature

Examination Title

Centre

Centre No.

Candidate No.

**Examination
Details**

0	0	0	0
1	1	1	1
2	2	2	2
3	3	3	3
4	4	4	4
5	5	5	5
6	6	6	6
7	7	7	7
8	8	8	8
9	9	9	9

Supervisor:

If the candidate is ABSENT or has WITHDRAWN shade here ▭

PET Paper 2 Listening Candidate Answer Sheet

You must transfer all your answers from the Listening Question Paper to this answer sheet.

Instructions

Use a PENCIL (B or HB).

Rub out any answer you want to change with an eraser.

For **Parts 1, 2** and **4**:
Mark ONE letter for each question.
For example, if you think **A** is the right answer to the
question, mark your answer sheet like this:

| 0 | A̶ | C |

For **Part 3**:
Write your answers clearly in the spaces next
to the numbers (14 to 19) like this:

| 0 | example |

Part 1		Part 2		Part 3		Do not write here		Part 4	
1	A B C	**8**	A B C	**14**		1 14 0		**20**	A B
2	A B C	**9**	A B C	**15**		1 15 0		**21**	A B
3	A B C	**10**	A B C	**16**		1 16 0		**22**	A B
4	A B C	**11**	A B C	**17**		1 17 0		**23**	A B
5	A B C	**12**	A B C	**18**		1 18 0		**24**	A B
6	A B C	**13**	A B C	**19**		1 19 0		**25**	A B
7	A B C								

Acknowledgements

The publishers are grateful to the following for permission to reproduce copyright material. It has not been possible to identify the sources of all the material used and in such cases the publishers would welcome information from copyright owners.

Voyages Jules Verne for the advertisement on p. 31; the extract on p. 52 is adapted from *Body and Soul* by Anita Roddick, copyright © 1991 by Body Shop International, PLC & Russell Miller. Used by permission of Crown Publishers, a division of Random House, Inc; Nene Valley Railway for the extract on p. 71.

The publishers are grateful to the following for permission to reproduce copyright photographs:

gettyimages/Taxi/TRAVELPIX for p. 11; Castle Mall, Norwich, for p. 51; © Martin Bond/Photofusion for p. 56.

Colour section
ImageState for p. II (1B); gettyimages/ImageBank/Real Life for p. II (2B); Powerstock/Zefa/DAMM for p. III (3B); Robert Harding Picture Library for p. III (4B) and p. VI (1C); gettyimages/Taxi/Denis Boissavy for p. VI (2C); gettyimages/ImageBank/Larry Dale Gordon for p. VII (3C); gettyimages/Stone/Penny Tweedie for p. VII (4C).

Picture research by Hilary Fletcher

Illustrations by Oxford Designers & Illustrators

Book design by Peter Ducker MSTD

Cover design by Dunne & Scully

The cassettes/CDs which accompany this book were recorded at Studio AVP, London.